PENGUIN BUSINESS
LEADERS PEOPLE LOVE

Yeo Chuen Chuen is a multi-award-winning leadership coach who has been honoured with international accolades for her outstanding work with clients in nearly forty countries across five continents. Named LinkedIn Top Voice in Company Culture (Singapore) in 2022, she has been recognized as an invaluable partner in offering accessible pathways to developing great leadership by shifting mindsets.

Having worked with senior executives from Fortune 500 and the Singapore Government Service since 2013, Chuen Chuen has demonstrated that a return to fundamentals—helping leaders lead from a state of strength, authenticity, and curiosity—is the secret to unlocking their fullest leadership potential. The strategic value she brings to her clients is proven with her long-term relationship with returning clients, referrals, and highly satisfied clients.

As one of the executives said about their work together, 'Chuen Chuen's programme is the only one leaders need to do.' Chuen Chuen finds great joy in designing training programmes, tailor-made to each unique organization she partners with. As a creator of simple but transformative frameworks, she has also created a proprietary Re4 Model, (documented in her book *8 Paradoxes of Leadership Agility*) as well as the Five Inner Voices you'll learn about in this book.

Connect with Chuen Chuen
1. ACESENCE.com: Join her email list at acesence.com/laf-subscribe
2. LinkedIn: linkedin.com/in/chuen-chuen-yeo.
3. Email: chuenchuen@acesence.com

T0049401

ADVANCE PRAISE FOR *LEADERS PEOPLE LOVE*

'In today's fast-paced, ever-changing workplace, agile leadership has become more critical than ever. *Leaders People Love* beautifully guides readers to navigate and adapt to modern leadership challenges to achieve even greater success at work. A must-read!'

—Brenda Bence
Ranked Top 10 Executive Coach Worldwide,
Thinkers50 World Leader in Coaching

'This book is fantastic for leaders committed to lead at their best. It offers practical strategies that overcome real-life challenges leaders face in a fast-changing world, enabling them to develop and empower teams effectively.'

—Frank Koo
Head of Talent Solutions Asia, LinkedIn

'The relatable and authentic examples, presented in an easy-to-understand manner will entice one to read on. I strongly recommend *Leaders People Love* to readers who appreciate a refreshing approach to learning key leadership concepts while understanding how to accentuate their strengths to become a leader people love.'

—Ronnie Lee
Director, Services Sales, Lenovo Greater Asia Pacific Region

'Chuen Chuen's book contains snippets from her conversations with business leaders. This book is probably the next best alternative to being coached by Chuen Chuen herself. Any leader who wants to avoid a plateau in their career should read this book and draw on her wisdom from working with global leaders.'

—Tang Li Chow
Deputy Director, Human Resources,
Singapore Institute of Technology

'As a founder-CEO I am a work in progress. I believe that all of us can become better leaders—leaders that are loved—if we are self-aware of our strengths and weaknesses. In the age of generative AI, what we need from our leaders will also change. When repetitive, technical tasks are taken over by machines, only human-to-human relationships will remain. If leaders everywhere can take to heart some of Chuen Chuen's lessons, such as empathic leadership, agility, storytelling and coaching, they will no doubt be ready for the change that awaits them.'

—Juliana M. Chan, Ph.D.
CEO, Wildtype Media Group
Publisher, *Asian Scientist Magazine*
Young Global Leader, World Economic Forum

'An easy and inspiring read for leaders who aspire to make a positive impact on workplace happiness and fulfilment. By weaving authentic storytelling, actionable insights and reflective questions for self-evaluation throughout the chapters, Chuen Chuen skilfully lays out a sound framework comprising five inner voices of agile leadership to engage people meaningfully. This book is a valuable guide to leaders in today's ever-evolving work environment with diverse teams.'

—Kathleen Seah
Head, Human Capital, PhillipCapital

'In the wake of the pandemic, challenges faced by teams are further exacerbated by rising expectations. Chuen Chuen's book couldn't have come at a better time. The current operating model of sacrificing personal needs to meet escalating job demands is unrealistic. This book holds many actionable strategies; leaders need to adopt the mindset to achieve fair equilibrium, prioritising the well-being of their employees, increasing satisfaction, engagement and productivity.'

—Amol Pradhan
Chief Transformation Officer
SIH Cloud Advisory and Enterprise Agility

'This book is a class apart with its simplicity. The framework and explanations are easy to grasp. Every leader, whether leading small or large teams, must read this book as it will equip them with the self-exploration, guidance and action required to become agile leaders that the world needs today and people would love to follow.'

—**Dr Lakshmi Ramachandran, PhD**
Career & Professional Development, Centre for Future-ready
Graduates, National University of Singapore
20+ Years in Life Sciences, Speaker, Coach (ICF & Belbin)

'What was shared in this book is easy to comprehend and I would go back to reading it over and over again to serve as a constant reminder to grow and be the leader that my people would love. *Leaders People Love* offers lots of practical leadership advice. The examples/stories shared herein made it all even easier to comprehend, especially for those newer to their leadership career.'

—**Sun Yoke Kuan**
Regional Sales Director, Enterprise ASEAN, Databricks

'*Leaders People Love* is a remarkable book on leadership—a true gem replete with practical insights and a deep emphasis on self-awareness. A must-read for anyone seeking to unleash their full potential and create a lasting impact in their organizations and communities.'

—**Jonas Lim**
Vice President of Solutions
Consulting (Asia Pacific and Japan), Pegasystems

'This book provides you the "legendary scroll" all leaders need. It invites you to see yourself, discover and tap into your deepest talents and unlock your fullest potential. I especially love the content of Section II, "Five Inner Voices of Agile Leadership". I enjoyed this part so much, including the quotes, and even tried memorizing some of them! *Leaders People Love* will give you insightful tips and actions based on both theory and practice.'

—**Fadly Rasyad**
Enterprise Agile Coach & Leadership Circle Practitioner,
Bank of Singapore

'I love how *Leaders People Love* delves into diverse facets of effective leadership. Replicating the practices of prior successful leaders may not necessarily lead to success in one's leadership pursuits. The book advocates for a continual process of self-evaluation, needing to reflect and align leadership styles with the needs of their team.'

—Grace Wong
Head of Finance and Operations, Swagelok Indonesia

'This book focuses on today's emerging themes, such as encouraging neurodiversity and building inclusive cultures. I love that Chuen Chuen has pushed for shifts in societal attitudes, beliefs and bias, starting with leaders in the workplace. In a world where there isn't a single normal, this book has given you—leaders—the permission to think differently and the power to bring about change.'

—Helen Fairchild
Chief Operating Officer at California Department
of Human Resources (CalHR)

'I love the analogies used and practical solutions/actions offered for self-reflection. It is an easily digestible read that empathises with the important concept of being an authentic, genuine leader who builds a great team through trust. The practical self-evaluation helps readers to broaden perspectives and use different "toolkits" to balance meeting employees' various needs whilst getting the best out of them.'

—Ang Sze Pheng
Director, HR APJ, Syniti

'A delicious read with a refreshing new take on leadership. I particularly enjoyed the self-evaluation questions that prompt you to reflect deeply about your own approach to leadership. Chuen Chuen has encapsulated the key competencies leaders need to equip themselves with through this book.'

—Vivek Iyyani
Multigenerational Workforce Speaker

'*Leaders People Love* gives you the insights, perspectives and tools you need to perform in a changing and volatile environment. The well-defined and accessible framework opens your mind to the state of leadership in today's world. The book asks some hard, probing questions on leadership, challenging your assumptions and understanding. Its words of wisdom and anecdotes bring the message home, reflecting on immediate application, and redefining your leadership style.'

—Andrew Shuttleworth
Head of Business Development, Asia Digital Lab,
Obayashi Corporation

'I love how this book covers almost everything from self-awareness as a leader, to how to inspire and influence your team through storytelling. This book will be relevant to you no matter the stage of your career. Aspiring leaders also need to read this to keep these agile leadership principles in mind to lead in their own right.'

—Rae Fung
Speaker, Speaking Coach, & Talkshow Host

Leaders People Love

The agile leader's guide to creating great workplaces and happy employees

Yeo Chuen Chuen

PENGUIN
BUSINESS

An imprint of Penguin Random House

PENGUIN BUSINESS

USA | Canada | UK | Ireland | Australia
New Zealand | India | South Africa | China | Southeast Asia

Penguin Business is part of the Penguin Random House group of companies
whose addresses can be found at global.penguinrandomhouse.com

Published by Penguin Random House SEA Pte Ltd
9, Changi South Street 3, Level 08-01,
Singapore 486361

First published in Penguin Business by Penguin Random House SEA 2023
Copyright © Yeo Chuen Chuen 2023

ISBN 9789815127973

Typeset in Garamond by MAP Systems, Bengaluru, India

www.penguin.sg

Contents

Foreword

We all know that a leader can make or break your day, and that leaders can make or break a business. In this time of increasingly rapid change, automation and artificial intelligence, we cannot forget that we are human. The people we lead are not just assets to the company or human capital. The people we lead are, in fact, people. People with thoughts, feelings, wirings, perspectives, passions, struggles, talents, needs, and ideas of their own. If we care about human potential and want people to flourish in addition to the bottom line, we owe it to ourselves and the people we lead, to do the inner work required to lead differently.

None of us set out to be ineffective leaders. Whether one is new to leading or seasoned in leadership, we are limited by the leadership models we've seen and the defaults we've adopted. The roles that we've previously held, would rarely have prepared us to lead. The strengths and skill sets required as an individual contributor are not effective predictors of leadership competency. Role models of great leadership are few and far between. Often, we don't want to lead like the people who led us, and we know the workforce these days doesn't want to be led that way either.

As leaders, we have the power to either support or silence the people we lead. If we simply tell people to work harder, faster and longer, we will inevitably burn them out. We will squash the very genius, creativity and insight we are looking to unleash. In contrast, if we are able to lead with human-centric ease and authenticity, we can support each person on our team to find their way, come up with novel solutions and show up with all the insight and energy they have to solve the challenging problems we collectively face.

The choice is ours. Let's choose to be leaders that people love.

Elaine Lin Hering
Managing Partner, Triad Consulting Group
Author, *Unlearning Silence: How to Speak Your Mind,*
Unleash Talent and Live More Fully

Prologue

Hope is a curious thing.

Many people I come across through my work have entered the workforce with hearts full of hope. Eyes bright and brimming with positivity, they had hoped the road ahead would be smooth and frictionless—a straight line to the prize at the top. They aspired for their talent to be noticed immediately, to be promptly recognized and soar above everyone else. That the corporate ladder would magically become an accelerated elevator for them and they would arrive rapidly, without resistance, at the top to make that significant mark, have an impact in the workplace, and maybe even on the world.

There is nothing wrong with having hope. It's in all of us as human beings to have desires, yearnings and dreams. We all dream of becoming bigger at the end of life than we had been at the beginning, after living a full and worthwhile life.

Hope is a curious thing. It keeps burning as long as we fuel it. It can burn defiantly in the face of resistance or the cold winds of disapproval; it may cool into glowing embers, but will likely never be completely extinguished unless one decides to give up on it altogether.

Over the years, as I partnered with leaders in private one-on-one coaching engagements or as a strategic adviser designing bespoke leadership programmes for their organizations and teams, I often saw this distinguishing mark in those designed to succeed—the refusal to give up hope.

Having sat in this ringside seat, I have had the privilege to witness and hear the undisguised, unfiltered thoughts and raw feelings that they rarely felt safe to share openly in any other forum. In the arena of senior leadership, vulnerability is perceived as a weakness.

I have reaped the benefits of having this front-row view as a neutral party. First, I feel honoured to be trusted and allowed into the inner circle as a worthy companion. Second, I treat it as a valuable privilege to see issues clearly without any camouflage, and to perceive the individuals as they are—in the light of their truth. Finally, even more valuable is the opportunity to uncover emerging patterns across organizations and formulate transformative solutions that can change lives and workplaces for the better.

In fact, over the years, I have noticed that some patterns repeat with predictable regularity. Some of these are perennial challenges with the potential to stunt organizational growth and erode the well-being of staff, while others pose a threat to the mental health and effectiveness of leaders and their achievements.

Once I noticed these recurring patterns, I had to turn these insights into usable and accessible tools. Not sharing these insights would mean doing the world disservice.

While the insights I share in this book have been gleaned from real-life scenarios I have encountered in my work spanning nearly forty countries, I will share them without disclosing the identities of the people involved, to honour the trust they placed in me.

In the final analysis, 'who' the stories are about does not matter as much as what you will derive from exploring the elevated mindset due to the agile leadership principles and strategies. This book is about you—the hopeful leader the world is waiting for.

I hope the strategies in this book will inspire you to be the leader the world needs today. With a new mindset and actionable insights, I believe you will feel more ready and equipped with the leadership competencies to turn chaos into opportunities, confusion into clarity, and fear into assurance. When you take action, you will become a leader that people come to love. While the road ahead may not always be clear, with calm, quiet confidence, and wise and sound strategy, you can and will succeed. I have high hopes for you.

Becoming a leader whom people love is a tall order. The road to transformation is not without its difficulties. In the fast-moving business climate, we want people to approach the hostile environment with excitement instead of fear. In an increasingly divisive world, we want people to band together despite being fundamentally different. In a world where all rules of success are ever-shifting, people must face the unknown with optimism, dare to fail, and try again. This book will present many mindsets that appear to go against the normal vein of thinking and education. But as you reshape many familiar paradigms—such as definitions of relationships, people, power, structures and systems, success, and impact—the new you can emerge. You will become more resilient and forge unique ways to succeed, even as the world morphs.

Keep your hope alive and the fire in your gut burning. The world is waiting for leaders who can revive purpose and meaning in work and joy into the lives of the workforce. Reach your fullest potential and make that most significant impact in your life as a leader.

May every workplace be led by leaders people love. That will be our greatest gift to humanity and the world.

Introduction

How this book came about

One of the questions I frequently ask as I hear people describe the gap between their desired and current states at coaching conversations is this: 'Given that you have tried and failed many times with this approach, why do you still repeat it?'

Eyes would glaze over and two blinks later—as if the question had triggered a mental reset—the answer would often be, 'Oh, I don't know why. I suppose I just didn't know any other way. I've not seen anyone try anything else.'

This is the issue—many leaders in the workplace are still operating based on an old script. Knowledgeable only in outdated approaches and assumptions whose validity has long expired, they are stuck in a loop of irrelevance that no longer delivers results. Yet, they remain hopeful that the strategies will one day work again.

Even though these approaches often stem from good intentions, they must be addressed. That's because these well-meaning but out-of-date actions can sometimes be so damaging that they quicken the widening of the rift between desired and current states, worsening matters instead of improving them.

It's like adding fuel to the fire when you mean to douse it. Here are some examples:

- When business leaders hope to erase differences in a diverse workforce through a one-time intervention or announcement, followed by a series of poorly executed and unempathetic moves. (As if a Big Bang announcement from someone with massive doses of charisma who is very high up in the food chain, or a perfectly performed speech would be enough to wipe out all resistance, doubt, and differences!)
- When leaders believe employees will continue to sacrifice their personal needs and goals to meet the increasing job demands.
- When they think raising the pay would increase productivity, people will keep delivering, crushing, and over-exceeding goals.
- When leaders stack initiatives one on top of another without 'cutting the fat', then scratch their heads in bewilderment when their workplaces are associated with a culture of poor mental health, stress, lack of psychological safety, burnout, and inability to retain talent.
- When a manager with the kindest intentions tries to help people grow and develop, but gives feedback that's perceived as non-constructive and harmful, hurting employees' morale and motivation to learn—and as a result, creates the exact opposite effect, destroying hard-earned trust and relationships.

The landscape has shifted, but leadership approaches are yet to catch up.

> 'Naïveté is doing the same thing over and over, and always expecting the same result.'
>
> Niels Bohr, Danish physicist

The crux of ineffective leadership is not the intentions but the consistently outdated approaches leaders have adopted, even though they have stopped delivering results. Many assumptions are no longer true and need to be re-examined.

For instance, consider some of the following.

a. **What does it mean to lead?**
- Are leaders thinkers and followers doers?
- Are leaders strong and followers weak?
- Are followers faceless, voiceless beings incapable of thinking for themselves; are leaders protectors who must make decisions for them on their behalf?
- Are leaders infallible beings who are know-alls, be-alls?

b. **What about the idea of 'right' solutions?**
- What does it mean when a solution is right? Right, for whom?
- What are the consequences of getting the solution wrong?
- What does it mean when someone proposes a 'wrong' solution?
- Is the state of being right or wrong permanent or transient?
- What is in between right and wrong solutions? Would any of these solutions be useful in certain circumstances?

c. **What is work?**
- Is it a way to earn a living? Is it all or part of life?
- Is work meant to fulfil a greater purpose as a collective? Where do the individual's purpose, meaning, desires, and dreams sit?
- Is work associated with or limited to a location?
- Where does the individual's identity rest?
- How is work supposed to feel? Stressful? Dehumanising? Forceful? Or uplifting and nurturing?

From the patterns I have spotted, these questions highlight just some of the assumptions that have rapidly faded into irrelevance, indicating an undeniable shift in what employees want. A large proportion of leaders are still not catching on, and the rift is widening. The solution, however, is within sight.

Leaders today can be so much more effective and inspiring if they go back to the foundation of what it means to be a human, first, and then an evolving, growing, agile entity, because:

We are constantly changing as we interact as members of a larger ecosystem.

We continuously receive feedback through our interactions, which are instrumental in helping us learn and change. Connecting with others within such an ecosystem offers us a chance to serve and co-create something meaningful. We each contribute in some way, leaving our footprints, making our legacies, shaping and moulding the ecosystem over time. Just as our human journey is centred around discovering ourselves and seeing ourselves more clearly, we can also help others see themselves more clearly.

If we rediscover what and how the ecosystem has changed and what it means to contribute to this living community, we will come one step closer to becoming effective leaders.

How to Use This Book

This book is divided into two sections:

Section I covers 'Agile Leadership Fundamentals' that will take you through reflective exercises to help you understand the changing ecosystem and redefine 'leadership' by reconstructing your leadership map. This section is sequential, so I encourage you to go from beginning to end.

Section II presents my proprietary leadership framework in the form of the 'Five Inner Voices of Agile Leadership'. I have developed this five-part framework over the years to help leaders strengthen each of the inner voices, namely:

- Captain
- Developer
- Strategist
- Visionary
- Agilist

Each inner voice is characterized by a mindset and overcomes a set of performance blocks I have encountered most regularly in my international practice spanning forty countries since 2017.

You will discover more about each inner voice in the corresponding chapters and why it's essential for you, given the trends of the future of work. Each sub-chapter is also further organized by themes. These themes have recurred often enough from my practice to warrant in-depth discussion. I will lay the groundwork and take you through multiple perspectives to arrive at mindset shifts that I believe will benefit you immensely. As a result, some themes are longer and more extensive, which is correlated to the frequency at which I have observed leaders grappling with them, so take your time with these.

You will also often find names of leaders featuring as characters to represent real people I support. As a reader, you now have the privilege to go behind the scenes with me, follow their journeys and watch their development unfold. At every juncture, I will highlight how each character has challenged and rewritten their old script. These will be indicated with 'Navigating the Conundrum'.

For most characters, you will follow the journey of mindset shifts from start to end, concluding with their success, which will be indicated with 'Outcomes'.

Strengthening all five inner voices will help you engage others and have a meaningful impact. It will also increase your integrity and authenticity as a person of influence.

This second section can be read in two ways:

- Sequentially, starting with the inner voice that interests you most.
- Thematically, beginning with the theme you view as most important.

To decide where to begin, take the Agile Leadership Superpower Quiz at https://leaderspeoplelove.com/resources or read up on the themes to see which is most relevant.

Take the Agile Leadership Superpower Quiz
at https://leaderspeoplelove.com/resources

This book is also written with busy leaders in mind; you will find focus notes that encourage you to take action, indicated by:

- **Self-evaluation:** A reflective or retrospective exercise to evaluate your present or form a deeper understanding of the topic. You can also find the digital version of the exercise on my website.
- **Key Points in a Snapshot:** The essence of learning points you can immediately act on.
- **Agile Leadership Pointers:** The foundational beliefs that will elevate your perspective.

I also frequently refer to golden nuggets from conversations with the guests on my podcast, *Agile Leaders Conversations*. You can listen to the full conversations and receive even more wisdom from these on my website (https://blog.acesence.com/category/agile-leaders-conversations/).

No matter how you choose to begin reading this book, my goal is to nudge you gently but powerfully to shift your mindset permanently. The world has changed and needs to be led by leaders with a relevant and up-to-date mindset—leaders like you! I hope this book will be your trusted companion for shaping new behaviours that will transform your leadership, attract inspiring results and outcomes, and steer you towards an elevated, truly purposeful life.

Let your journey begin!

Section I

Agile Leadership Fundamentals

1

Agile Leadership

Future-Proofing Your Career and Life

During my work as an executive coach and leadership consultant, I have come across many types of leaders. Some stand out for their clear and futuristic thinking, others for their desire to teach others what they have learned so they too may succeed. Most of these leaders are highly talented and have illustrious careers, but many eventually reach an uncomfortable plateau.

> 'In a hierarchy, every employee tends to rise to his level of incompetence.'
>
> Laurence J. Peter and Raymond Hull,
> *The Peter Principle: Why Things Always Go Wrong*

According to *The Peter Principle*, every person who becomes competent in their current job would earn a promotion, gaining access to another job that requires different skills. If the person learns the new skills and proves competent, they will be promoted again to the next job level.

Suppose the unfortunate event does occur when the person finally reaches a point where they are not able to learn the required skills and become permanently incompetent. In that case, they will get stuck at the last placement—a place termed 'Peter's Plateau'. This is a level beyond which leaders cannot rise in their existing systems, officially becoming stuck.

Stuck [v.]: *To be or remain in a place or situation; be unable to progress, change or improve despite one's best efforts, often resulting in frustration and confusion.*

Undeniably, given all their talents, every leader with an intrinsic motivation to thrive and learn should be concerned if they begin to feel stuck. Getting stuck is no fun at all, for often, it means a person is too senior to play a junior role (this damages the ego and pride) and too incompetent to play a larger role. In my view, however, getting stuck is normal, even for high performers.

That's because even as they strive to expand their skill set and attain overall success while nurturing a healthy level of hunger, the world around them continues to evolve at a breakneck pace, increasing in complexity and uncertainty, sometimes outpacing their ability to catch up.

So, despite their best efforts to adapt and evolve, leaders may not see the expected results. Internal pressure builds as these leaders realize that the strategies that have worked wonders in the past are no longer effective. Whatever they had been doing might now hardly be enough to keep them afloat or help them stay ahead.

This uncomfortable phenomenon is a valuable symptom that indicates that change is needed. Once leaders get this wake-up call, it usually motivates them to seek external support and guidance, to break patterns and change habits, which usually kickstarts our work together. Their desire to figure out how to achieve success sustainably is common, and this is where agile leadership (and I) enter the picture.

As we begin the discovery process, many questions swirl in their minds:

- What does it mean to be agile so they can always keep up?
- What are the boundaries and limitations of agility?
- What's a better way to live, work, and succeed?
- Where and how can they begin?
- How can they sustain the process?

Some found the process of self-discovery uncomfortable and confrontational, while others were thrilled and excited. Their responses depended on their original frames of reference about life, work, leadership, and success and how far removed these ideas were from the harsh reality.

There are usually two groups of leaders and responses.

The first group are leaders accustomed to a top-down and rigid management system, and are not used to defining their own criteria for leadership and success. They are far more used to being handed a rubric by the organization (or their reporting officers) and given the mission to meet all the criteria and check all the boxes. Their discomfort is understandable, for they have been used to a system of management that's not accustomed to agility. To make this clearer, let's look at these two quotes.

> 'We will never transform the prevailing system of management without transforming our prevailing system of education. They are the same system.'
>
> 'The relationship between the student and the teacher is identically the same relationship as between the subordinate and the boss.'
>
> Dr W. Edwards Deming, as quoted in
> Peter M. Senge's *The Fifth Discipline*

Such leaders often wonder why the 'good ol' rules' no longer work. They have a hard time understanding new ways of working and leading.

The second group of leaders are more open to learning and new experiences. They may have experienced other systems of management or education. These leaders tend to be more optimistic and excited about learning new things. For them, all that remains is to address the above questions on agility and redefine their compasses.

Fortunately, the process I have detailed in this book applies to both groups of leaders.

Whichever group you belong to, one thing remains clear—the world will keep changing. The choice is yours—whether to change, adapt, or remain the same. Regardless of how you respond, there's a cost involved.

'The agility comes in every phase of your work as your status changes. It begins as something intriguing, something unfamiliar, and one thing is clear—what has worked for you in the past is not going to work anymore because the world is changing. I encourage all leaders to jump on the bus because the worst is to stand still and get left behind.'

An excerpt from Episode 8, *Agile Leaders Conversations* with Ronnie Lee, Director, Services Sales, Lenovo Greater Asia Pacific Region

---

Agile leadership is not a destination but a way of life and leadership. Keep an open mind, always check your mindset, and you will remain agile.

What is Agile Leadership?

Simply put, it's the ability to navigate complexities and uncertainties with a sense of ease and authenticity. It's the innate quality to continuously observe the connections between people, environment and situations, and draw meaningful insights that enable you to grow, evolve, and improve. It's the undeniable quality of staying relevant and effective no matter how your context changes.

Agile leaders are characterized by the mindset always to observe and introspect, notice and course-correct, unlearn and relearn—all with consistency and purpose—to prevent the undesirable outcome of obsolescence and irrelevance.

In this section, I will take you through the process of discovering the agile leader within you, step by step. This process is iterative, so I recommend that you revisit it from time to time. It will help you delve deeper into what defines you. Like peeling the layers of the onion, you will discover something new about yourself each time you do it.

Other than self-discovery, this process also often restores joy for my coachees—many of them mature, seasoned professionals. While perceived as highly successful, many of them have been experiencing increasing tensions that have compounded into deep dissatisfaction. This state, commonly described as a 'lack of integrity' where the inner and outer worlds are misaligned, is often caused by rapid external change but slow internal growth. With the process, you too can expect a state of integrity to return, restoring joy and increasing motivation. For my coachees, they were once again primed to make an even bigger impact on their professional ecosystem.

'The privilege of a lifetime is to become who you truly are.'

Carl Jung

I hope this process will help you re-understand and renew yourself, invite possibilities, and maximize your impact.

Agile Leadership Pointers

Agile leadership is not a destination but a way of life and leadership that prevents obsolescence and irrelevance.

Self-Evaluation

- Which group of leaders do you belong to, the first or second group?
- Where in your life do you feel stuck? In which areas are you doing very well and leading with relevance?
- How do you generally feel when it comes to uncertainties and complexities?
- What assumptions and beliefs might need to be challenged and refreshed?
- What new beliefs can you invite to be more receptive to possibilities and ways of thinking?

Please refer to https://leaderspeoplelove.com/resources
for the digital exercise.

Your Reflections

Which group of leaders do you belong to, the first or second group?
Where in your life do you feel stuck? In which areas are you doing very well and leading with relevance?
How do you generally feel when it comes to uncertainties and complexities?
What assumptions and beliefs might need to be challenged and refreshed?
What new beliefs can you invite to be more receptive to possibilities and ways of thinking?

2

Construct Your Leadership Map

> 'Don't go outside your house to see flowers. My friend, don't bother with that excursion. Inside your body there are flowers. One flower has a thousand petals. That will do for a place to sit. Sitting there you will have a glimpse of beauty inside the body and out of it, before gardens and after gardens.'
>
> Translated by Robert Bly, *Kabir: Ecstatic Poems*

A leadership map, in my definition, is a blueprint for a leader. It undergirds all the decisions one makes at home, in the workplace, and in all other aspects of life—for clarity, I believe work is a subset of life and does not constitute all of life. The map describes where the leader is headed directionally, what he would love to do more of, whom he wants to collaborate with, the causes he feels passionate about, and at the end of life, how he measures his life and contributions.

Without a relevant map, we lose our sense of direction and have a scant idea of how we define success or what will bring us happiness and joy. Consequently, we may feel directionless, confused, and exhausted by work and life. Not having a map is like peddling on a bicycle with all your might, only to realize at the end of the journey that you have been moving in the wrong direction, have arrived at the wrong destination, and are too exhausted to return and start over.

You may have heard of once-dynamic individuals who were the envy of others. But their souls were depleted along the way and they could no longer taste happiness because their senses had become too numb. They might eventually realize that meeting others' expectations and fulfilling others' dreams generated happiness felt only by others and not by themselves. They slogged hard, only to reach the *ultimate anti-climax* of their lives.

A leadership map is essential if you want a life of satisfaction, joy, and fulfilment. To begin uncovering your leadership map, complete the following self-evaluation.

Self-Evaluation

- What principles are consistent across your work/life?
- What is success?
- What are the core pillars of your life and work?
- What makes you, you?
- What's meaningful and makes your soul sing with joy?

Your Reflections

What principles are consistent across your work/life?

What is success?

What are the core pillars of your life and work?

What makes you, you?

What's meaningful and makes your soul sing with joy?

2.1. Your Success Formula

Years ago, I worked with Penny, a senior director who wanted to increase her influence and ability to bring about changes. When I asked her what would make our engagement successful, she replied without missing a beat, 'I want you to give me the formula that will turn me into the inspirational leader I know I am destined to be.'

I can appreciate her desire to be efficient—if we know a foolproof way to reach the goal quickly, why not take it? After all, as the saying goes, leaders are made, not born. This thinking, however, while generally true, is also the cause of many leaders' struggles today. Why do I say this?

Believing that great leadership can be learned, has its merits, but it has also misguided people into thinking there is a secret fixed formula for great leadership. That was likely why Penny had hoped I could deliver the formula straight into her hands.

Honestly, I love the passion and drive of leaders. Their hunger to learn and find their best possible self is what makes them high-potentials. Their positive energy is infectious!

But over the years, I have seen that what distinguishes those who truly rise and transform from those who don't, is their choice—whether they continue seeking an external solution or find the courage to go on an inner journey. In fact, whenever I see these leaders, they always remind me of the movie *Kung Fu Panda*.

2.2. The Panda's Reflection

For the sake of this discussion and to make a long story short, I will focus on three elements of the movie's story—the mysterious scroll, the snow leopard, and the panda.

First, the scroll.

It was no ordinary scroll. It was the dragon scroll, a scroll containing legendary martial arts secrets that had remained hidden for thousands of years, awaiting the appearance of the prophesied Dragon Warrior—the bravest of the brave; the most skilful warrior in all the land. He was to be the one who had proven himself worthy after successfully overcoming many trials and hardships.

Enter the snow leopard, Tai Lung.

Driven mad by his failure to be chosen as the Dragon Warrior, even after enduring the most gruelling training and suffering the greatest pains, he was left caged in a dungeon, guarded by thousands of highly skilled warriors. He was deemed unworthy despite his obvious prowess.

Case in point: **Superb skills don't automatically make one fit to lead. Being right and being number one in terms of technical skills don't make one ready to lead.**

Let's pause and take a look at ourselves. Wasn't there a time in our lives when, like Tai Lung, we trained hard to become skilful so that anyone could see that we were *worthy* of being a great leader—the best leader, the Dragon Warrior?

In pursuing great leadership and success, sometimes the drive can become an intense desire. If we ignore the feedback in the form of resistance and obstacles, and keep pushing ourselves to move in the wrong direction, then indeed, it's possible to drive ourselves to madness. That is how people get themselves stuck.

Agile Leadership Pointers

Ignoring feedback and being blind to the signs is a sure way to get stuck, deep and fast.

So, for the leaders I work with, I first help them understand that if they want to become great leaders relevant to today's workplaces, they need to be less like Tai Lung.

Skills are important, as are intelligence and cognitive ability. But soft skills— human, cultural, emotional, and contextual awareness—are even more so, especially in today's diverse workplaces.

But if not the skilful, capable Tai Lung, then who? This is where the panda, Po, comes in. It was clumsy and unremarkable Po with a body full of hidden talents, who eventually became the Dragon Warrior. Po applied himself diligently and consistently, and overcame many obstacles to be the one to obtain the scroll finally.

Then came the climax.

As Po held the legendary scroll between his paws and opened it with trembling hands and glittering eyes, the scroll glowed with a mysterious golden light to reveal . . . himself! For there was absolutely nothing inside the dragon scroll except a golden mirror. All the panda saw was his reflection.

So, dear leader (and reader)—the first ingredient of effective agile leadership is to know yourself. Instead of looking outside for a formula, you must begin the search within.

Key Points in a Snapshot

- Hard skills are important but can only get you so far. Soft skills make a significant difference in the later stretches.
- Everyone leads successfully in their unique ways. Instead of a one-size-fits-all attitude, strive to discover your style.
- Navigating complexities and uncertainties with authenticity and a sense of ease can only be achieved when you lead from your heart.

2.3. Step One: Inside-Out Discovery

Now, let us get back to Penny, the senior director on the quest to become a great leader. In our conversation—which I remember as clearly as if it had just happened yesterday—she was animatedly sharing her grand plans and the obstacles she wanted to overcome.

To help Penny begin her inner journey, I invited her to construct her leadership map by asking herself a few questions, starting with: **What is leadership?**

'What is leadership?' I asked.

The first response I got was pin-drop silence. It was as if the floodgates of her thoughts had suddenly clammed shut as Penny struggled to find words to express her understanding of the word 'leadership'.

It was certainly not because the question was beyond Penny's ability—for it was not a matter of intelligence—but rather because it was the first time someone had cared enough to ask her about her personal aspirations, desires, and wishes as a leader. She had been stuck and fossilizing in an ancient and obsolete system, where her sole duty was to meet the criteria for success handed to her by people of higher authority.

If you are reading this and are also stumped by the void of silence in your mind, fret not. **It's not too late.** No matter where you are on your leadership journey—whether you're new or a veteran, fresh or seasoned—you can begin right where you are by answering the following self-evaluation questions. These questions are also available in the Leadership Agility Force, a membership site for aspiring agile leaders, which you can sign up for at https://leaderspeoplelove.com/resources and find more resources there to help you on your journey. Also check out other exercises on the website, including Leader of Impact exercise, Values exercise, and strengths assessment.

Some might feel these questions are frivolous, but not Penny. She had felt stuck long enough to realize that something fundamental wasn't right with the way she approached matters, so she decided to do the work and that yielded gems of realization.

Some people still believe leaders are born, while others believe leaders are made. Maybe it's both. But one thing is clear.

Agile Leadership Pointers

If you don't know what you are made of, then the best version of you cannot be born.

Great leaders are authentic and real. They are not afraid to give their best to the world, even if it means showing their true selves.

Key Points in a Snapshot

- Instead of letting others define good leadership, define it for yourself.
- Authentic, agile leadership is deeply aligned with your values and strengths.
- Personal mastery and self-awareness are essential qualities of agile leaders.

Self-Evaluation

- What is leadership?
- What values guide you?
- What are your strengths?
- Where and how do you contribute your strengths in a meaningful way that will make your heart sing?
- What is that result, effect, or contribution—both tangible and intangible— that will make your life and career feel worthwhile?

Your Reflections

What is leadership?

What values guide you?

What are your strengths?

Where and how do you contribute your strengths in a meaningful way that will make your heart sing?

What is that result, effect, or contribution—both tangible and intangible—that will make your life and career feel worthwhile?

2.4. Step Two: Outside-In Scan

Soon, Penny discovered her own definitions of her core values and her view of what purposeful and meaningful contribution as an authentic leader looked like. Once she uncovered her talents and the types of work that brought out the best in her, her inner compass was ready. Having completed the first part of the puzzle of effective, agile leadership, and after her inside-out journey of discovery, Penny was ready to begin the second part of the process, an outside-in scan.

This second part, the outside-in process, is about collecting evidence to validate the relevance of your leadership map and then evaluating the effectiveness of your actions and approaches. This part will also inform you if you need to update or refresh your leadership map, bringing you back to refine your findings from Step One.

It's not enough to rely only on 'what makes you tick', or on your authenticity, because a 'stubborn' and 'wilful' leader is often someone who is just being true to themselves. This is also a key learning point derived from the paradox of 'principled versus adaptable', mentioned in my book, *8 Paradoxes of Leadership Agility* (2020). This paradox describes the tension between being so principled that one becomes inflexibly stubborn, and being so highly adaptable that one lacks a compass or moral code—or in other words, a backbone.

> *A highly authentic leader who is irrelevant*
> *is as good as an ineffective or bad leader.*

If you have been working doubly hard but getting disproportionally unremarkable results, it's a clear sign that you need to complete an outside-in scan. Through this, the truth you want to discover will shed light on the following for you:

- Is what you can and want to give to the world relevant and appreciated?
- Are you indeed a great leader, or a bad boss wearing the skin of a good one?

The truth is, you will never know the answers to these questions until you draw meaningful insights from evidence and feedback. That's why this second half of the puzzle is so important—it requires courage and humility. It requires you to apply the ability to observe and learn—a critical hallmark of an agile leader.

The ultimate goal of this uncomfortable process is to get yourself out of the 'self-deception' box, as described by Arbinger Institute.

> 'Self-deception is like this. It blinds us to the true causes of problems, and once we're blind, all the "solutions" we can think of will actually make matters worse. Whether at work or at home, self-deception obscures the truth about ourselves, corrupts our view of others and our circumstances, and inhibits our ability to make wise and helpful decisions.'
>
> Arbinger Institute, *Leadership and Self-Deception: Getting Out of the Box*

To guide Penny through this second part of constructing her leadership map, I introduced my Re4 Model and its four steps.

Four steps of the Re4 Coaching Model

STEP 1
RECONSTRUCT THE MAP

An unbiased, courageous reality check, leading to
a recognition of the truths in the context, which
are likely different from how they were initially
perceived.

STEP 2
REFRESH THE LENS

Uncover and weed out biases, prejudices, or
over-generalized rules that are no longer effective,
leading to an internal shift of mindset.

STEP 3
RENEW THE IDENTITY

The shift is made explicit. It comes alive as the
individual entrenches it using an anchoring
metaphor that points to a new persona.

STEP 4
REBUILD THE CAPABILITIES

New skills and actions are learned, acquired, and
practiced, leading to improved outcomes.

Now all Penny had to do was complete these steps of the Re4 Model, starting with reconstructing the map.

Below are the questions she answered for her outside-in self-evaluation.

Self-Evaluation

Individual Observations

- How do people react to you or regard you, in general?
- Did any of their responses or reactions surprise you? If so, why?
- How accurately do people read your intentions when you operate in the workplace? Are you often misunderstood, or are people unsure about your intentions?
- What areas were you moving the needle in the direction you intended, and in which areas were you moving in the opposing direction?

Stakeholder Interviews

- Pick three to five stakeholders (people who collaborate with you regularly *and* people who are courageous to speak the truth because they want you to succeed).
- What do people say about you when you are not in the room? Ask your stakeholders to use three adjectives or short phrases to describe you.
- What is one piece of advice each stakeholder has for you to improve your results immediately?
- Ask for one suggestion each from your selected stakeholders that you can consider implementing.

This first and most important step of reconstructing the map, was expectedly uncomfortable for Penny, as it felt confronting and disorienting. Sometimes, we claim that we want to hear the truth but the truth might feel too hard to handle. The stakeholder interviews were helpful as Penny discovered quite a few gaps between her self-perception and how others perceived her. Seeing her slightly deflated, I encouraged her to face feedback objectively. After all, the gaps she discovered were opportunities to develop new understanding and acquire new learnings.

If you find yourself fearing stakeholder interviews, don't. Approach them with courage, for they could help reveal your 'moments of truth' that might reverse your course from ineffective to effective leadership. It can even change your career trajectory. It can elevate your impact to a whole new level and the discomfort will be worth it in the end.

The hard truth can be as searing as lasers.
You could get scorched or burnt.
But it can also be your warm guiding lamp that illuminates the right path.

Key Points in a Snapshot

- Authenticity alone is not effective because relevance is key.
- Only your stakeholders and the responses within your ecosystem can inform you about your relevance.
- Use the outside-in scan to uncover the gaps between your perception and reality.
- Return to step one whenever necessary.

I encourage you to undertake the self-evaluation Penny answered for herself, along with insights obtained from your own stakeholder interviews, and record your observations in the space provided.

Your Reflections (Self-Evaluation)

How do people react to you or regard you, in general?
Did any of their responses or reactions surprise you? If so, why?
How accurately do people read your intentions when you operate in the workplace? Are you often misunderstood, or are people unsure about your intentions?
What areas were you moving the needle in the direction you intended, and in which areas were you moving in the opposing direction?

3

Leading after the Hyperbole

'We simply have to work doubly hard and faster until we find the right people to fill the positions,' is a comment I hear often.

Many leaders I work with face increasing pressures to deliver greater results while working with diminished resources. Naturally, as we begin to explore strategies to cope with the demand, we instinctively want to 'just bite the bullet' and follow orders.

I usually offer an alternative view: 'I get that everyone is very hardworking and that results are important. I'm curious . . . How long can people work at that kind of pace and speed? In other words, how sustainable is it?'

While we can all understand the pressing need to deliver results, we must not ignore the fact that conditions are often not ideal. So, given the volatile conditions where all rules are constantly broken and assumptions from hypothetical case studies are rarely true, how sustainable is it to keep pushing for speed, quality, and volume when resources are diminishing?

'If something cannot go on forever, it will stop.'

Stein's Law by Herbert Stein, Economist

When I raise the topic of sustainability, I highlight five aspects of the broader context for decision-makers to consider.

1. Energy and food
2. Population
3. Talent deficit
4. Workforce needs across generations
5. Total well-being

3.1. Energy and Food

According to an article published in *American Scientist*, energy and food costs have risen since 2002. World energy expenditure has also been steadily rising from its low point around 1998, exacerbated by the fact that we are literally using energy to create energy. In sum, the cost of producing energy and food was at its lowest around 2000, after which it steadily rose. (Wing 2017)

Given the planet has limited resources, the pressure to source cleaner and greener ways to generate energy is immense. Until we see clearer solutions to meet the rising energy demands, energy and food will become progressively more expensive. Although there is speculation about whether supplies of oil and metal are indeed being depleted (Kirsch 2020), much of the attention today is devoted to finding solutions to sustain our way of life.

Key Points in a Snapshot

Energy and food costs are expected to rise until sustainable and clean energy sources are found.

3.2. Population

Population growth, while slower every year since 1968, is causing a decrease in cost–benefit ratio. Supporting the same population with rising energy and food costs has become more expensive. Plus, the population is ageing, causing a rise in the dependency ratio. This means it will be more difficult for economically productive workers to support those who are not. The smaller dependency ratio from the 1960s (where the number of economically productive workers was higher than non-workers), has now reversed. Since 2010, the number of non-workers has outnumbered workers.

Leaders seeking to expand their headcount to meet rising demands inevitably feel the impact of this demographic trend, as it becomes more challenging to hire and fill all the positions required.

Key Points in a Snapshot

- The number of non-workers has surpassed the number of workers since 2010, increasing the demand for workers to support non-workers.
- It's now more challenging to replace workers.

3.3. Talent Deficit

A report by Korn Ferry estimated that by 2030, there would be a worldwide talent shortage of 85 million people (Binvel et al 2018). This deficit was further aggravated by the COVID-19 economic shock beginning in 2020. In the labour market, half of all employees worldwide might need reskilling by 2025. To address this, the Reskilling Revolution, an initiative launched by the World Economic Forum, aims to reach 1 billion people with future-ready skills, better education and opportunities, by 2030.

But it's not only technical and cognitive skills that we need to look at. In addition to green and digital skills often highlighted in skills gap reports, McKinsey also named '56 foundational distinct elements of talent' (abbreviated as DELTAs) that people will need in the future for work (Dondi et al 2021). These foundational skills and attitudes are categorised across four domains:

- Cognitive
- Interpersonal
- Self-leadership
- Digital

In this book, I focus on the intrapersonal skills and attitudes categorised under 'self-leadership' and interpersonal skills, such as inspiring trust, empathy, motivating different personalities and resolving conflicts. These are skills commonly highlighted as requirements for effective leadership.

Here are three noteworthy findings from the study conducted by McKinsey:

1. There is **lower than average proficiency** in 'Communication' and 'Planning and ways of working'.
   Communication comprises the DELTAs:
   - Storytelling and public speaking
   - Asking the right questions
   - Synthesising messages
   - Active listening
   Planning and ways of working comprise the DELTAs:
   - Work-plan development
   - Time management and prioritisation
   - Agile thinking
2. There was **no obvious link between education level and proficiency** in many DELTAs within the self-leadership and interpersonal categories, such as:
   - Self-confidence
   - Coping with uncertainty
   - Courage and risk-taking
   - Empathy
   - Coaching
   - Resolving conflicts
3. There was a **negative correlation between education and DELTAs like humility and inspiring trust**—suggesting that highly educated individuals score lower in these two DELTAs, which many would agree are crucial for leaders today.

Key Points in a Snapshot

- There is a global shortage of people with adequate skills.
- It will take time and intentional commitment of resources to upskill them.
- Leaders need to gain some core competencies today, such as communication, storytelling, and agile thinking.
- There is no link between education level and proficiency in essential leadership qualities like empathy, self-confidence, courage, and risk-taking.
- Based on McKinsey's findings, high education could be negatively correlated with highly valued qualities like humility and inspiring trust.

Self-Evaluation

- How have you allocated time and resources to develop the skills and attitudes needed to lead effectively?
- Between hard and soft skills, which rank higher for you?
- Of the DELTAs named by McKinsey, which ones do you have gaps in? Which ones are your natural strengths?
- Refer to the list of DELTAs mentioned in the preceding section. Do the above trends apply to you? What follow-up actions are due?

Your Reflections

How have you allocated time and resources to develop the skills and attitudes needed to lead effectively?

Between hard and soft skills, which rank higher for you?

Of the DELTAs named by McKinsey, which ones do you have gaps in? Which ones are your natural strengths?

Refer to the list of DELTAs mentioned in the preceding section. Do the above trends apply to you? What follow-up actions are due?

3.4. Workforce Needs across Generations

The future of work holds great potential for a more diverse workforce with new opportunities in the job market. There is increasing focus on the widening gap between the 'haves' and the 'have nots', changing the way businesses need to operate to create better work and more equitable societies.

Advances in technology and shifting social attitudes are changing the way companies hire. Where the employee pool might have been restricted to a geographic location in the past, organizations can now hire from virtually any part of the world. This is a positive development in light of the talent shortage, but it also presents challenges to managers seeking to foster the right conditions for collaboration.

Over the past years, multiple trends created by employees seeking better lives after COVID-19 have also emerged. These may not be new to you:

- The Great Resignation
- The Great Reshuffling
- Quiet Quitting
- The Great Betrayal

These are just some of the many trending catchphrases that often capture news headlines. Decision-makers might be tempted to dismiss them as 'much ado about nothing', but my suggestion is that they listen carefully, for these are voices of the workforce.

Agile Leadership Pointers

Always listen to the wind and catch the whispers before they grow into howls.

To comprehend the underlying message the trends indicate, I strongly encourage you to consider and study them. Use the self-evaluation at the end of this chapter and you might find something relevant and insightful to aid you in this process.

Increasing diversity in the workforce is also bringing profound changes to the workplace. According to the Good Work Framework, a whitepaper published in May 2022 by World Economic Forum, millennials and Gen Z workers will make up 72 per cent of the world's workforce by 2029, 20 per cent higher than the 52 per cent in 2019. It is, therefore, crucial to understand the needs of millennials and Generation Z, while not forgetting those of the earlier generations.

With rising life expectancy and older retirement age, leaders could easily manage four, sometimes five generations in the workplace. This is why we need to understand the generations, what is important to each of them, and how to motivate and engage them. Leaders have the added responsibility to foster intergenerational understanding if we want to draw out the best results.

Fortunately, many studies have been done by organizations globally, presenting useful insights to help leaders appreciate the differences and uniqueness of their diverse workforce.

Here is an overview of the general trends for each generation bracket. Bear in mind that the patterns are presented to help leaders make better guesses about the needs of employees. However, each employee is unique; **nothing beats having a personal conversation to understand how to engage and motivate them** so that you can tailor your leadership styles and managerial practices for the best results.

Generational Trends

Baby Boomers (1946–1964)

They want employers who, in order of priority (O'Boyle 2023),

- are ethical
- care about their well-being

They are also financially stable and spend a median of 8.25 years working in a job (Marcellus 2021).

Gen X (1965–1980)

They want employers who, in order of priority (O'Boyle 2023),

- are ethical
- care about their well-being

They are also financially stable and spend a median of 5.17 years working in a job (Marcellus 2021).

Millennials (1981–1994)

They want employers who, in order of priority (O'Boyle 2023),

- care about their well-being
- are ethical
- are open and transparent

They spend a median of 2.75 years working in a job (Marcellus 2021). They are also mobile pioneers—meaning, though the internet was new, they were young enough to adapt.

Younger millennials are digital natives, and have a higher level of debt and lower real assets. They value pay and benefits, flexibility and work-life balance, and personal and professional growth (Deloitte 2021).

Gen Z (1995–2012)

They want employers who, in order of priority (O'Boyle 2023),

- care about their well-being
- are ethical
- are inclusive[*]

They spend a median of 2.25 years working in a job (Marcellus 2021).

Gen Zs are digital natives—they cannot remember a time without the internet. They are risk-averse, thrifty, and optimistic, likely because, like the Silent Generation (the generation before Baby Boomers), Gen Zs grew up during a period of severe economic decline (Quillen 2020). They feel strongly about racial, gender, and sexual-orientation equality issues, and prefer brands that align with their values (O'Brien 2017). Gen Zs cite empowering work culture and potential for career growth as the two most important factors in a job (Desjardins 2019). They

---

[*] Younger millennials and Gen Zs ranked this point over open and transparent leadership.

are highly likely to demand personalization of their career journeys (Gomez et al 2023).

General Employee Trends

Further noteworthy studies have uncovered other trends.

Better Opportunities

An upskilling study by Amazon in 2022 found that skills development is a top priority for 83 per cent of the 3,000 employees surveyed. Among those surveyed, 78 per cent fear they don't have the skills needed to advance their careers, 58 per cent are concerned their skills are not up-to-date, and '70 per cent feel unprepared for the future of work' (Schawbel 2023).

Around two-thirds of employees also indicated that they are inclined to leave their jobs in 2023 if there is a lack of growth opportunities, and join another company that offers better opportunities. This number jumps to almost three-quarters among Millennials and Gen Z workers.

The report highlights the three types of growth opportunities employees seek as follows:

- Skills development
- Career advancement
- Transitioning into a new role or career path.

In addition to skills development, the report also highlighted other motivations people have when they seek new roles:

- Higher pay (59 per cent)
- Better work-life balance (48 per cent)
- Better sense of purpose (41 per cent).

Hybrid work

Another trend is hybrid work. Rare in the past, this is now one of the top priorities for many, particularly younger jobseekers. Managing remote workers and fostering team collaboration puts additional pressure on leaders, requiring them to perform differently and gain new skills.

A separate report by McKinsey indicates that the intention to resign is up globally and 65 per cent of people who left their jobs between 2020–2022 have not returned to the same industry, further debunking employers' popular belief that employees can be easily replaced with someone with similar skills and experience (Smet et al 2022).

Traditionalist vs non-traditionalist

In the same report by McKinsey, the employee pool was further split into two pools: traditionalist and non-traditionalist.

Traditionalists are career-oriented people who care about work-life balance but are willing to make trade-offs for the sake of their jobs. They are motivated to work full-time for large companies in return for a competitive compensation package and perks, a good job title, status at the company, and career advancement.

What attracts traditionalists to jobs:

- Career development and advancement
- Adequate total compensation
- Meaningful work
- Workplace flexibility
- Reliable and supportive people at work
- Traditionalists may be easily found and attracted through common recruitment strategies, but they do not exist in high enough numbers to fill all the jobs.

The non-traditionalist group includes students, gig workers, the self-employed, caregivers, etc. The ranked factors that attract each sub-group of non-traditionalists vary, but they share the following in common:

- Workplace flexibility
- Meaningful work
- Adequate total compensation
- Support for health and well-being
- Career development/advancement

Key Points in a Snapshot

- Millennials and Gen Z workers will make up 72 per cent of the world's workforce by 2029.
- Different generations have different needs.
- Emphasis on equality in pay, gender, and healthcare, and alignment with personal values are on the rise.
- Meaningful work, career development, personal growth, workplace flexibility, and adequate total compensation are generally of rising importance.
- Employees join new industries more often, increasing the chances of replacing every employee lost with someone of similar experience and skills.

Self-Evaluation

- What do the trends indicate?
- How do the trends affect you, your team, and the organization?
- What future trends can you identify?
- How well do you understand what drives your team?
- How do you measure your current level of relevance on a scale of 1 to 10? (10 for the best)
- What shifts are needed now for you to lead with greater relevance and higher impact?

Your Reflections

What do the trends indicate?
How do the trends affect you, your team, and the organization?
What future trends can you identify?
How well do you understand what drives your team?
How do you measure your current level of relevance on a scale of 1 to 10? (10 for the best)
What shifts are needed now for you to lead with greater relevance and higher impact?

3.5. Total Well-Being Engaging the Whole Person

Traumatic events often disrupt our core beliefs and challenge our assumptions about safety, the order of the world and our future. In recent years, the COVID-19 pandemic created an unprecedented global disruption. As the world goes through post-traumatic growth (Tedeschi 2022), the pandemic's continued influence on people's wants and ideals is reshaping workplace norms and dynamics. The post-COVID workforce now wants different things from work and life. For many, that difficult season might have spurred a greater appreciation for life (and reconsiderations as to where work fits into the scheme of things) or inspired them to value existing relationships more.

Changing Perceptions about Work

According to the Mercer Global Talent Trends 2023 report, the pandemic has changed the way people think about work, with a few noteworthy patterns (Bonic et al 2022):

- More people want to work less and have greater work-life balance.
- More people see work primarily as a means to an end (pay cheque).
- The percentage of people who felt at risk of burnout has increased, with Gen Z (89 per cent) and millennials (89 per cent) being most at risk of burnout, compared to Gen X (78 per cent).
- Percentage of people who felt energized at work fell, with Gen Z being the least energized and millennials being the most energized.

Rising Stress Levels

Well-being has become a primary focus for many, with multiple studies indicating that stress levels have increased since the pandemic.

According to the State of the Global Workplace Study 2022 by Gallup, stress has reached another all-time high globally, with 44 per cent of respondents indicating they experienced 'a lot of stress the previous day', compared to 43 per cent in the past year. Stress and burnout experienced by middle managers have also increased since the pandemic started, and the widening of stress and burnout level between senior leaders (22 per cent) and middle managers (35 per cent) in 2021, is both intriguing and concerning (Harter 2021).

Increasing Focus on Well-Being

The upside is that workplace leaders are paying attention to the trend data. From the Mercer Global Talent Trends Report 2023, more organizations have stepped up on total well-being initiatives recently than in previous years: 'executives believe that total well-being is the workforce initiative that would deliver the second-highest business results (second only to reskilling)' (Bonic et al 2022).

Shifting Expectations of Businesses' Roles in Society

Stakeholders' expectations of businesses have also shifted. The Annual Trust Survey conducted by Edelman in 2022 indicated that trust in governments has been declining over the years. While businesses are more trusted by people, with greater trust, comes higher expectation.

The public now expects businesses to take the lead in addressing societal problems on climate change, economic inequality, and workforce reskilling—areas in which governments were perceived to have done too little. The 2023 Annual Trust Survey by Edelman, however, noted that businesses face added complications in taking on social issues, especially when 'engaging in contentious issues', and may risk becoming politicized.

Meeting stakeholders' expectations by contributing positively to societal issues, however, could be potentially rewarding for businesses. Results from the 2022 Edelman study also indicated that brands or employers who demonstrate beliefs and values aligned with the general public's beliefs and values could benefit from higher consumer advocacy, attracting talent and investment.

Culture of Care

Organizations today face greater pressure to safeguard the total well-being of their workforce by not only taking care of the physical and mental well-being of workers in their organizations, and also actively working to close the equity gaps in income, provide access to high-quality healthcare, etc. Leaders need to shape and cultivate a supportive and caring environment for consumers and employees, as well as hyper-personalize their benefits to attract and retain talent.

Key Points in a Snapshot

- The world is seeing post-traumatic growth, changing the relationship between work and life, with more wanting to work less and enjoy greater work-life balance.
- Burnout and risk of burnout are on the rise among Gen Z and Millennials.
- Stress and burnout experienced by middle managers are also increasing; the stress and burnout level between senior leaders and middle managers is widening.
- Overall, optimism towards life is falling along with the collapse of economic optimism.
- More organizations have stepped up on total well-being for employees, with executives believing that total well-being is the workforce initiative that could deliver the second-highest business results, after reskilling.

Refer to https://leaderspeoplelove.com/resources
for more tools and strategies.

4

What it Takes for Leaders to Make an Impact in Today's Workplaces

Scanning the landscape and returning to the question of leadership sustainability, the period moving forward can only be expected to be more disruptive. Gone are the days when organizations could pick and choose employees to fill positions from amidst a rich and deep talent pool with the right skills and attitudes. Talent, once gone, is not as easily replaced or even found. In this landscape, leaders in the workplace will continue to face enormous pressures with diminishing resources, as they are expected to lead their teams to achieve ever-increasing results.

Managers and leaders in every workplace need to equip themselves with the mindset and skill set needed to transform workplaces. Beyond just 'getting the job done', leaders must engage and empower employees to do their best work. Work also needs to be meaningful and aligned with the needs of a diverse workforce. On top of that, leaders have to ensure their teams are well taken care of—in terms of physical, mental, emotional, and financial well-being—while also taking care of themselves. All this, they must accomplish against the global backdrop of division, polarization, distrust, and instability.

A lot now rests on the shoulders of leaders and managers. This can be both frightening and exciting. Although the road ahead may seem daunting, I believe your efforts to increase your agility will pay off. As you aspire to become a highly effective and relevant leader, use the outside-in scan to fully understand the need of the people you lead.

Self-Evaluation

- How many of the trends presented above are already within your awareness?
- What else are you noticing that's not stated?
- What skills and attitudes do you need to develop so you will be relevant, agile, and effective?

Your Reflections

How many of the trends presented above are already within your awareness?

What else are you noticing that's not stated?

What skills and attitudes do you need to develop so you will be relevant, agile, and effective?

4.1. Global Survey Findings on Leaders People Love

Study: Correlation between Happiness at Work and Managerial Effectiveness

Before writing this book, I wanted to find out if there is a correlation between happiness experienced at work and managerial effectiveness. So I decided to design and conduct a survey named the 'Leaders People Love Global Survey'. At the time of publication, this survey has spanned across fifteen countries, collecting responses from working professionals ranging from Baby Boomers to Gen Z, all levels of seniority and responsibility, as well as fourteen job functions. The purpose of the global survey was to test out my hypothesis:

Happiness experienced by employees at work is positively correlated with manager effectiveness.

To keep things simple, I did not distinguish between the various definitions of 'happiness' and 'joy' in this study. What makes each person happy differs, so a broad understanding of happiness would suffice for the purpose of the survey. Similarly, I used the words 'manager' and 'leader' synonymously.

The first part of the survey focuses on factors that would increase employee happiness. Specifically, I wanted to know what else besides managerial effectiveness would increase happiness. This would include organizational factors like work culture. Next, I also wanted to nail down what behaviours are perceived as effective management.

The second part of the survey aimed to capture the perceived level of disruption experienced by an individual and the associated readiness of managers to lead during disruptive times. Through this second part, I was interested in discovering the competencies people believe managers need the most so that they can lead effectively during disruptive times.

Fundamentally, if managers have the right mindset and understanding of people's needs, then at a minimum, they can create conditions so that work:

- is a rewarding experience despite its challenges, uncertainty and volatility due to ongoing disruption;

- offers a chance for people to put their best talents to use, often entering a state of flow that evokes joy.

'Everything rises and falls on leadership.'

Dr John C. Maxwell, World's No. 1 Leadership Guru

State of Flow

Introduced in the 1970s by Mihaly Csikszentmihalyi, the concept of the state of flow encompasses a mental state in which a person performing an activity is fully immersed in a feeling of energized focus, performing an activity that's challenging enough and stretches the person's capacity to perform. People who experience this state of flow report a heightened sense of well-being, fulfilment, and joy. The most interesting observation was that the flow state was **more easily attained at work** than at leisure (Biasutti 2011); it's a key that unlocks performance and happiness. I believe leaders people love play an important role in enabling this state of mind.

The data collected over the months indicates a positive correlation between happiness experienced at work and managerial effectiveness. This means managers are instrumental to changing lives. This alone makes it a worthwhile investment to become a leader people love.

Please note that this survey is still ongoing and these are the results as on the date of publication of the book. You may refer to leaderspeoplelove.com for the most up-to-date results.

Happiness and Managerial Competencies

From the survey, 87.4 per cent of respondents agreed that their happiness level at work is affected by their immediate manager's leadership effectiveness, of which 72.8 per cent 'strongly agree'.

On top of leadership effectiveness, respondents were asked to select all the factors that affected their happiness at work. Here are the factors and percentage of respondents who selected them.

- Personal growth (72.3 per cent)
- Culture (71.4 per cent)
- Salary (65.6 per cent)

- Career progression (62.7 per cent)
- Flexible work (56.9 per cent)
- Work friends (52.5 per cent)
- Organizational purpose (47.1 per cent)

Given that respondents picked many factors, the trend indicates that employees' needs have expanded. Hence, leaders need to understand the teams, hyper-personalize and lead with greater agility.

The next thing I wanted to uncover from the survey were the specific behaviours that would increase happiness at work. Respondents were asked to pick a maximum of three desirable behaviours. Of the various managerial behaviours mentioned in the survey, a few stood out:

- Recognizes me for my work (52.3 per cent)
- Trusts me to do my best (40.1 per cent)
- Cares about me as a person (35.6 per cent)
- Empowers me to do work my way (34.2 per cent)
- Provides clarity and sense of direction (32.5 per cent)
- Challenges and enables me to grow (27.7 per cent)
- Considers my views, even when they are opposing (24.3 per cent)
- Develops my career (22.6 per cent)

The range of responses also indicates that different people need to be led using different means, with emotional elements ranking higher than hygiene factors, underscoring the need for leaders to change their leadership styles.

One size no longer fits all but rather fits only one.

Managerial Competencies Needed to Lead in Disruptive Times

When asked about the 'level of disruption' faced in their jobs, around 13.6 per cent of respondents indicated that they were facing little to no disruption. Conversely, the remaining respondents indicated they were facing disruptions, with nearly 61.8 per cent of respondents rating the level of disruption as 'very high'.

When asked about the effectiveness of managers in navigating disruption, around 62 per cent of respondents rated their managers as effective, out of which only 27.6 per cent rated their managers as 'very effective'. Conversely, 17.2 per cent of people rated their managers as 'very ineffective'.

Given the high correlation between happiness and managerial effectiveness, we can deduce that when managers are not equipped to lead in times of disruption effectively, more employees will likely be unhappy at work. Imagine a workplace where nearly 40 per cent of your colleagues are unhappy. Given the importance of trusting and good relationships to many people, I believe working in an environment as described above would induce quite a high level of stress in me, to be honest.

4.2. Five Inner Voices of Agile Leadership

To rise to a higher level of effectiveness, leaders now need a different roadmap. This leads to the question I am often asked:

What does effective leadership in today's workplaces even look like?

To answer this question, I formulated the 'Five Inner Voices of Agile Leadership', a framework designed to help leaders navigate the changed world through tangible steps. I explain them in detail in the following pages. In some sections, you will find mindset shifts that immediately illuminate your path. In others, you will find ways to enhance your understanding of common managerial behaviours and how you can perform better. As you learn about the Five Inner Voices of Agile Leadership, you will find leadership lessons organized by theme, that will change how you approach common leadership conundrums and resolve them.

This five-part agile leadership framework will equip all leaders in highly complex and volatile workplaces, leading diverse and increasingly polarised workforces to achieve meaningful goals beneficial for the world.

Enjoy your exploration and uncover the path to truly become an agile leader!

Agile Leadership Pointers

Agile leaders adopt a wide range of methods to engage and lead others, hyper-personalizing their methods to meet people's needs.

Key Points in a Snapshot

- Happiness at work is positively correlated with managerial effectiveness.
- Happiness evoked through the state of flow is more easily experienced through work than leisure.
- A range of other factors is important, indicating that people are motivated by different factors, further emphasizing the need for leaders to hyper-personalize their managerial approaches and be agile.

Section II

Five Inner Voices of Agile Leadership

THE CAPTAIN

BE SELF-AWARE SO YOU CAN BE
OTHERS-AWARE

One of the most impactful articles I have read on leadership is 'What Makes a Leader', published in *Harvard Business Review* in 2004, written by Daniel Goleman, the 'father' of Emotional Intelligence. He wrote:

'The most effective leaders are alike in one crucial way: They all have a high degree of what has come to be known as emotional intelligence. It's not that IQ and technical skills are irrelevant. They do matter, but mainly as 'threshold capabilities'; that is, they are the entry-level requirements for executive positions. But my research, along with other recent studies, clearly shows that emotional intelligence is the sine qua non (essential) of leadership.'

Having tripped over many obstacles and stumbled many times in my career, I cannot agree more. Despite being technically strong and guided by positive moral values, I have learned after being 'burnt' many times, that being good—hardworking, kind, and upright—is not enough to ensure success. The rules of engagement vary with context and dealing with the often-invisible norms of interaction with diverse audiences demands a much higher level of sensitivity to successfully connect and influence individuals.

Emotional intelligence and personal mastery have become even more important in our times.

Agile Leadership Pointers

Emotional intelligence and personal mastery are of increasing importance in creating diverse and inclusive workplaces.

5

Why the Captain Is a Leader People Love

Personal mastery is the core idea of the Captain. It's at the heart of what it means to be a good leader. The Captain believes that everyone brings value to the table and regards others with *unconditional positive regard.*

Without the Captain, everything else we discuss the other inner voices will serve merely as learned tactics and techniques. Leading with the Captain elevates the way a leader interacts with people. Most importantly, strengthening the Captain will improve your relationship with yourself—perhaps the most important relationship of all.

The Captain is particularly skilled in creating high-performing teams where team members complement one another. Naturally, with more understanding, empathy, and respect for what makes others unique, he leads with high emotional intelligence, building an inclusive team culture by ensuring the psychological safety necessary for agile teams navigating complexities in today's workplaces.

Refer to https://leaderspeoplelove.com/resources
for more Tools and Strategies.

6

Meet Jane

A Dynamic Stellar Performer Turned People Manager with Whom No One Wanted to Work

She was smart, talented, and dynamic.

Naturally, Jane easily differentiated herself as the best-performing member and was rapidly promoted to team leader. But just as quickly as her rise to stardom, things started going south when her team members departed one by one.

A series of exit interviews and dip-stick surveys were conducted to discover the issue. Then came the bad news. Jane, eager to make an impact in the next milestone of her career, had turned the heat up on her team members so much that each of them, desiring more freedom, empowerment, and enablement, decided they could not—would not—accept Jane as their leader. They felt stifled, shut down, and dismissed. Unknown to her, Jane's leadership style had created a toxic work environment.

Her team members did not want to be mini-Janes. Instead, they wanted to be known for who they were—Adrian, Tiong Han, Mongkut, Rashid, Deva, etc.

This is one of the more common scripts I see playing out and repeating across organizations. Like a broken record on repeat, poor team management plagues many enterprises, regardless of culture, geography, or industry after they promote the best-performing member to be the manager. Although the idea of empowering the workforce is not new, I rarely come across a leader who is able to wield an empowering leadership style with elegance and just the right amount of finesse and sensitivity. Workplaces are complex, and people are, too, after all.

Usually, how people are promoted to leadership positions remains the same—ineffective. High performers promoted to leadership positions are often left on their own to interpret what it means to lead, and what the corresponding success means. Role modelling is such a powerful way to shape behaviours and especially so in leadership. Not having the right role models can be both dangerous and limiting for younger and newer leaders.

Jane was without a predecessor or any healthy role models who could exemplify for her what a human-centred approach to leadership, or empowerment and enablement, looks like. She only had familiar ways to rely on, and in many cases, these are limited to rigid, outdated methods such as:

- Instructing/Telling
- Directing
- Repeating/Nagging

If you have read the findings above on what the workforce wants, you will immediately see why this way of leading is ineffective. Stubbornly repeating what doesn't work will only increase the rifts between employees and leaders.

My work with Jane was centred on first salvaging the situation and then significantly improving her managerial competencies. We had to work on smoothening her rough edges before her team completely disappeared, because if she ended up in a position where she had no followers, she would hardly be able to call herself a leader, let alone grow as one.

Key Points in a Snapshot

- The lack of positive role models limits agility among up-and-coming leaders.
- Methods like instructing, telling, directing, and repeating are ineffective for employees today.

7

Theme I: Encouraging Neurodiversity and Inclusion

Neurodiversity has become increasingly important and beneficial in workplaces today, offering solutions to problems many businesses face—a shrinking labour force and talent pool, and the need for diversity of thoughts and ideas for better innovation.

While neurodiversity is not a new concept in the field of psychology and mental health, leaders shaping workplaces must also recognize that people's brains are structured differently, view these differences through the right lens, and then celebrate differences as strengths. Neurodiversity acknowledges that individuals with varying neurological differences can bring unique perspectives to society and businesses, increase innovation and add a competitive advantage (Mahto et al 2022).

Increasing acceptance of different thinking or learning styles, creating inclusive workplaces by fostering empathy and understanding, and providing greater access to resources and customized support for individuals, are some areas leaders can begin to explore. Such recognition can encourage creativity by embracing different kinds of thinking and opening up new ideas and perspectives that may not have otherwise been considered.

Neurodiversity has been linked to many positive outcomes, such as increased creativity, innovation, problem-solving skills, and productivity. Fostering an inclusive culture in the workplace will promote collaboration among neuro-diverse individuals who have the potential to come up with better solutions to complex problems. By embracing neurodiversity, organizations can benefit from the unique perspectives each individual brings to their team.

As leaders people love, the road towards truly inclusive workplaces where diversity is celebrated begins first with your own mindset.

7.1. Your Way Is Not the Only Way

'I seriously don't understand what I'm doing wrong. All I did was tell my team to repeat my exact formula and steps. Those are my precious trade secrets that I took years to discover. Instead of appreciating me, they are unhappy? How hard is it to repeat my steps?' Jane was seriously deflated and at her wits' end.

I can understand her frustration. The issue was not with her intentions or the end goal, but the faulty script in her head guiding all her actions.

From our sessions together, we uncovered some of Jane's unspoken beliefs:

- 'If I can do it, others can do it too.'
- 'I have the success formula; all that needs to be done is for others to repeat my formula for guaranteed success.'
- 'Business targets are the most important.'
- 'If anyone can't perform the steps in my formula, then they must be incompetent.'

To offer a different perspective, I shared the following story with her.

The Sad Boy Playing a Jolly Tune

Many moons ago, I was an accomplished pianist who harboured a dream of becoming a concert pianist, so I could make music and perform for a living. Part of that desire was seeded by my parents. Both had to leave school in their teens due to family circumstances, and learning music was a luxury they could not afford. So as a daughter on whom the parents had pinned their hopes, I committed myself to being a good pianist. I was the perfect daughter—diligent, persevering, and resilient.

I'm not sure if my passion for music was nurtured or innate, but as an adult, I saw the many benefits of an education in music. Once, I did a job suitability assessment and the results showed that both my left and right brains were equally 'strong'. According to the consultant, that was rare. I attributed this to my music education.

Now as a parent, I want the best for my children and decided that they too, must learn music, especially the piano.

'Well, since their mother was a quick learner and was rather skilful with the instrument, surely my boys would breeze through and excel in the domain too,' I thought to myself, feeling rather smug and confident. But alas! Nothing was further from the truth and the walls of harsh reality soon came crashing on me. My boys struggled with the instrument. Their fingers were not as dexterous as mine, and their hand-eye coordination was far less superior. Their little, short and stubby fingers hit the wrong black and white keys more often than the right ones, creating clashing chords of dissonance instead of soothing melodies.

For the next two years, I gradually turned from a kind, nurturing mother into 'mum-zilla'. The awful, clashing, discordant sounds wailing out of the instrument rudely violated my code of what it meant to make music and brought out the worst in me.

Before learning the piano, the young boys would always run to the door to welcome me home with whoops of joy as their favourite female adult figure showered them with hugs and kisses. After starting piano lessons, my appearance at the door would strike fear into their hearts, for they would instead be greeted with a torrent of demands and threats.

'Have you practised on the piano today? Why haven't you done it? You had better start now,' had become my 'welcome speech', each question articulated at a higher pitch and volume than the one before, sounding terse and furious.

Without my noticing, our mother–son relationship changed and that was not the only thing that deteriorated. My arrival at home would spark high stress and tension, quickly escalating into flared tempers, tears from the children, and a moody evening. It damaged our home dynamics and soured the atmosphere. But I persevered—like any good pianist would—through hours of daily practice. I wanted my children to enjoy the same benefits I had tasted from training as a diligent and skilled pianist. This goal was too important and too sacred to be given up. 'I shall not be a weakling,' I steeled my resolve.

Years later, I saw a scene that changed my perspective completely. As usual, my eldest was at the piano and I was 'coaching' him. The temperature was fast rising as I was barking my dissatisfaction in a shrill voice—'you played the wrong note AGAIN', 'why can't you play that passage correctly?' and 'how many times do I have to tell you?' After many failed attempts, he finally got the melody right. So I sat back, intending to savour the fruits of my labour with pride and enjoy the beautiful melody, but what I saw next made me pause. Tears were rolling down my boy's cheeks as his fingers played a happy and jolly tune on the piano. The dissonance between the visual and audio images was so unsettling that it hit me so hard and made me question the effectiveness of my methods.

What had I achieved?

What had I really done in the name of good intentions?

Had my behaviour damaged my children and our relationship?

What I had dreamt I would achieve, faced with the solemn reality, could not be further apart. The difference was so jarring that it created enough energy for me to finally tear up the script guiding my actions for years. This experience as a parent rewrote my beliefs. It changed me as a leader, too.

As I share this not-so-glorious story about motherhood and leadership with Jane, she too, fell silent, for she realized her approach had been counterproductive to her effectiveness as a leader. Instead of helping her team succeed, she was destroying her team from the inside. She was the enemy stopping a great team from doing their best work.

Agile Leadership Pointers

Just because you can do something doesn't mean others can, too. Everyone has a unique formula for success.

Replacing Beliefs

For both of us, we replaced our beliefs with something more relevant to our circumstances. Learning to play the piano gave me many valuable life lessons and qualities, but others may be able to receive the same benefits through other means.

My formula for success works only for me and others will have their own personalized success formula. The results are important, but the process is even more so. In the case of my children, our relationship matters more. For Jane, the atmosphere she created at work mattered more, because it directly impacted employee engagement and hence, her business results.

'The real inspiration is not to be the flame, but to enable others to ignite theirs.'

An excerpt from Episode 14, *Agile Leaders Conversations* with Frederic Ducros, Chief Transformation Officer, Malaysia

I am talented at playing the piano and my children are not me. They have talents in other areas. Similarly for Jane, she was talented in getting results one way, while her team could achieve results through other means.

Everyone has a spark waiting to be ignited—how will you ignite it?

Turning the focus back to you now. As you move forward with this new understanding, consider the next set of self-evaluation questions.

Self-Evaluation

- What is your role as a leader? Turn others into mini-you or something else?
- Could an unfamiliar way actually be a better way?
- What does "the right way" mean, anyway?
- How have you encouraged others to explore alternative ways of moving forward other than the one you know?
- When did you last listen to someone's ideas and consider them seriously?
- What affirmations might you give to encourage others to lean more into what they are naturally good at?
- How do you even begin to notice the glimpse of brilliance and genius in others?

Your Reflections

What is your role as a leader? Turn others into mini-you or something else?

Could an unfamiliar way actually be a better way?

What does "the right way" mean, anyway?

How have you encouraged others to explore alternative ways of moving forward other than the one you know?

When did you last listen to someone's ideas and consider them seriously?

What affirmations might you give to encourage others to lean more into what they are naturally good at?

How do you even begin to notice the glimpse of brilliance and genius in others?

7.2. Differences Are Advantages

'I just can't understand why people are so different from me!' Jane griped, irritation creasing her forehead. My reply to her was, 'I can see how getting people to see your point of view is important to you. I'm wondering, what would the world be like if everyone was exactly the same as you? Wouldn't it be shocking?'

Agile Leadership Pointers

Suspend your judgement on differences, for they are natural variations in a neurodiverse workforce.

- Human beings are naturally vastly different due to our genetic make-up. Add cultural, educational, and experiential differences to the mix—certainly, the world is a big melting pot of diversity.
- Different lenses and belief systems lead to different perspectives on the same issue.
- Different ways of analysing and dissecting an issue lead to different ways of solving a problem.
- Different preferences and operating modes lead to different ways of working.

Today's complex workplaces, where physical boundaries are permeable, offer golden opportunities for bringing diverse ideas, perspectives and solutions together.

Diversity Brings Business Advantages

Studies have consistently shown that diversity in the workplace, including at leadership levels, has a positive impact on profitability. The third report in a McKinsey series based on a data set captured from more than 1,000 large companies across fifteen countries, 'Diversity Wins', stated that 'top-quartile companies outperformed those in the fourth one by 34 per cent in profitability', with the 'likelihood of outperformance higher for diversity in ethnicity than for gender' (Dixon et al 2020).

The business benefits of diversity are clear. The differences in a diverse workforce are advantages that lead to greater profitability, especially when the organizational culture makes them so. It's up to agile leaders to harness the benefits.

A Neutral Point of View

In my observation, what often stands in the way of truly diverse and inclusive cultures at a fundamental level, is often the meaning people attribute to differences. It's usually judgement and labels that get in the way. In Jane's case, once she understood there was more than one way to get to the goal, the next step was to help her see differences from a neutral point of view.

What would it be like if differences were simply what they are—different ways of looking at the same picture?

There isn't a good, bad, kind, evil—but rather plainly, only not the same. The benefits of detaching differences from unhelpful labels like 'stubborn', 'uncooperative', or 'wrong', go a long way. Such labels are often the spark that ignites conflicts and disagreements. A LinkedIn poll conducted in 2022 by Harvard Business Publishing Corporate Learning asked individuals how people in their organizations responded when faced with conflict. This was what they reported witnessing:

- Blaming (36 per cent)
- Shying away (16 per cent)
- Listening to each other and sharing perspectives (28 per cent)
- Focusing on areas of agreement (19 per cent)

From the poll, we can see that 'blaming' is the most prevalent behaviour, and the precursor to that is often negative labels.

The positive side is that when employees learn the skills and attitude to work through conflict effectively, they may 'experience up to 30 per cent improvement in work quality, 40 per cent increase in productivity and near 50 per cent decrease in costs' (Harvard Business Publishing 2023).

Learning to deal with difficult interactions and personality differences is rewarding, because what organizations need today more than ever, is not the absence of conflicts, but productive ones. For productive conflicts to take place without casualties and hurting feelings, leaders have an instrumental role to play. Nurturing such an environment begins with your perception towards differences.

Self-Evaluation

- When someone sees a situation differently from you, what is your first reaction?
- Do you tend to gravitate towards and prefer people who think, feel, and act like you? What are the pros and cons of surrounding yourself with people similar to you in the long run?
- How have you subconsciously created an in-group and out-group? Is it beneficial or harmful to your team and organization?

Your Reflections

When someone sees a situation differently from you, what is your first reaction?

Do you tend to gravitate towards and prefer people who think, feel, and act like you? What are the pros and cons of surrounding yourself with people similar to you in the long run?

How have you subconsciously created an in-group and out-group? Is it beneficial or harmful to your team and organization?

7.3. Office Politics Are Merely Different Motivators at Play

I often meet people who feel tormented by office politics, so as I was planning this book, I felt this topic warranted some attention.

What is office politics?

Is it a power play? Tactics to outwit and beat others to be the first to get to the prize? All these could be right. But here is another truth about office politics: it's so very common. Put three people together and you get politics immediately.

Leaders today have the power and responsibility to shape organizational cultures that encourage innovation, constructive debate, and productive conflicts. Knowing how people naturally react to differences, you now have a choice as to how you would like to contextualise and navigate office politics.

It will be easier for us to normalise 'differences' as unique characteristics of individuals if we can accept that people will always

- have different motivations;
- view success at work and in life differently;
- have a different relationship with and understanding of power, status, and influence.

When we accept that those with whom we work will always have different perspectives and see the world a little differently—even if their view is slightly nuanced somehow—we can regard politics as an aspect of human-to-human dynamics, which is perfectly normal.

Key Points in a Snapshot

- A neurodiverse workforce offers different pathways to achieve positive results. These may not be the same as yours and may be in no way inferior.
- Differences are simply differences—not necessarily aggression, antagonism, or opposition.
- Diversity brings business advantages.

To navigate this topic of office politics with fewer grievances and more ease, consider the following questions.

Self-Evaluation

- How well do you know what motivates people with whom you work?
- Behind their every word and action, what drives them?
- Especially when matters get escalated and defence/aggression mechanisms are triggered, what is the real need for each individual?
- How can you respond with empathy, meet those needs, and foster more common ground for collaboration?
- If you, too, refuse to be embroiled in office politics, what are the guiding principles you can abide by as you create the right environment for your team?

Your Reflections

How well do you know what motivates people with whom you work?
Behind their every word and action, what drives them?
Especially when matters get escalated and defence/aggression mechanisms are triggered, what is the real need for each individual?
How can you respond with empathy, meet those needs, and foster more common ground for collaboration?
If you, too, refuse to be embroiled in office politics, what are the guiding principles you can abide by as you create the right environment for your team?

Theme II: Building Psychological Safety in Workplaces

In the following sections, we will explore how you can build psychological safety at the workplace so that people can bring their best selves to work.

8.1. Your First Response to an Unexpected Thought Matters

Have you ever wondered why some people rarely ask questions? Or answer so sparsely or safely when asked for their opinions?

Communication is only effective when there is two-way traffic. In a diverse setting with myriad ways to analyse and dissect the same situation, it's even more important for communication to achieve its true purpose—expanding perspectives that lead to a better solution.

Agile Leadership Pointers

The true purpose of communication is drawing from varying ideas to find a superior solution.

Psychological Safety

In this process, when unexpected thoughts emerge, the leader's first response to the new thought makes or breaks psychological safety. When people see harsh criticism being levied on an unusual thought or question, it will only create an environment where people would withhold their real thoughts. There's no question that they have an opinion—they simply don't feel safe enough to voice it. Similarly, if only opinions that align with the leader's feel welcomed, one can only expect people to parrot 'what the boss wants to hear' or share sanitized, politically correct opinions.

> 'Psychological safety—the belief that one can speak up without the risk of punishment or humiliation—has been well established as a critical driver of high-quality decision making, healthy group dynamics and interpersonal relationships, greater innovation, and more effective execution in organizations.'
>
> Amy C. Edmondson and Mark Mortensen,
> *The Fearless Organisation: Creating Psychological Safety in the Workplace for Learning, Innovation, and Growth*

In the global survey on Leaders People Love, we have found that among people who felt less happy at work, 'rude and transactional communication' ranked fourth among behaviours that eroded their happiness.

Navigating Jane's Conundrum

Returning to Jane, in helping her engage her team better, we deep-dived into one of the bits of feedback she received—people felt intimidated by her.

While many of her colleagues performed similar roles in other organizations, the protocol and how work was conducted in this organization were quite different. Often, Jane would give instructions and ask her team if they had any questions, only to be met with awkward silence. People would leave the meeting room as soon as possible, as if they were itching to escape. Typically, Jane would later discover that they did not understand her instructions at all and had been going in circles, doing everything except clarifying with her. If this happened once, it was perhaps a chance occurrence. Twice? Perhaps a coincidence. Thrice and more? It was a discernible pattern, and it needed to be addressed.

In our sessions, Jane's body language had so much to reveal. Depending on what she was talking about, she would exhibit different energies.

Sometimes she would be kind and warm, listening and responding thoughtfully. Other times, she would frown, the corners of her mouth turning downwards, her speech sounding terse and assertive. At times, she seemed passionate and serious, but those moments were quite intense even for me as a neutral party, looking in from the outside. I reflected at Jane my observations about the range of energies I was picking up from her. I wondered what her team's experience was, interacting with her five days a week over several events.

That was also when Jane realized she had been running a tight ship, at times insisting on *how* things should be done under the pressure of tight deadlines, and had come across as rude and transactional, possibly also dismissive and impatient.

In the global survey, we also found that people who were less happy at work had also indicated 'Micromanages and dictates how I do my work' as the most important behaviour exhibited by their managers that had the most negative impact on their happiness level.

In response to my observations, Jane shared that she remembered a few new joiners being more unrestrained and open to asking questions, but after a few short weeks, their questions also dried up. As Jane went into greater detail about how conversations usually evolved, she noted that one of them would ask a 'seemingly simplistic' question—one that she expected them to know the answer to already—and she would berate them for it, retaliating with questions served with looks of disapproval.

'What do you mean by that?!'

'Why do you think like this?'

'You should already know this.'

'How could you ask a question like that? That's what a newbie would ask. You are not a newbie.'

'Think before you speak!'

From Jane's responses, people quickly got the memo that unless they shared Jane's view and sounded knowledgeable enough, it was safer for them to keep quiet. Stupid questions were not allowed under Jane's watch.

We all know enough about communication to understand that it's only effective when there is a two-way dialogue. When meetings become a monologue where only the manager speaks, communication ceases.

'The biggest concern for any organization should be when their most passionate people become quiet.'

Tim McClure, Professional Speaker,
Brand and Leadership Consultant

Each of Jane's team members had experienced her high efficiency and deep knowledge in a similar way. Initially, they were excited to be able to learn from someone so capable, but once they experienced her harsh mannerisms, they no longer felt safe enough to ask questions or to share opposing ideas as they would be quickly shot down.

When people feel there is no space for any opinions other than the manager's, over time, even the most eager voice will fall silent. At team meetings, the only voice left was Jane's own, but in the informal meetings that took place after that meeting, real conversations flowed freely. Jane had no clue how her team felt and only realized there were problems when, one after another, her team members resigned.

> 'The worst kind of report leaders can get today is the watermelon report—green on the outside, red on the inside.'
>
> An excerpt from Episode 10, *Agile Leaders Conversations* with Sunil Mundra, Organizational Transformation Consultant, ThoughtWorks, Singapore

Evaluate your current leadership practices and identify ways to foster more psychological safety through the next exercise.

Self-Evaluation

- How forthcoming and open are people towards you?
- How do you encourage people to share their true thoughts and feelings, even the controversial ones, without fear of being judged, labelled, and blamed?
- Notice the effect of your behaviour on others. How might you shift your behaviour so that there is more curiosity, openness, and psychological safety?

Your Reflections

How forthcoming and open are people towards you?

How do you encourage people to share their true thoughts and feelings, even the controversial ones, without fear of being judged, labelled, and blamed?

Notice the effect of your behaviour on others. How might you shift your behaviour so that there is more curiosity, openness, and psychological safety?

8.2. Trust as a Leadership Brand

Many years ago, my colleague and I worked on a project. All was fine until she wasn't comfortable with a decision I thought we had made together. She decided to speak to our boss. My boss then called me into his office and said empathetically, 'I know how passionate you are, but you have to involve your colleague in the decision-making'. I was annoyed because I had no clue she was upset or had any concerns, for she had given nothing away during our discussions. I kept my composure and nodded stiffly.

As I left my boss's office, rigid with anger at the injustice, I found my colleague standing outside, waiting to pounce on me. The moment she saw me emerge with anger on my face, she took a deep breath and then started, 'So Chuen Chuen, I believe I need to be direct. So I went to our boss . . .'

That's a sure way to destroy trust—saying you are guided by a certain value and then behaving in the exact opposite way.

Building Trust

How do you build trust? Is it by being collaborative, friendly, and hardworking? Or by fulfilling your promises, being supportive, and ensuring everyone has a voice? Whichever way you build trust, one thing is clear. Trust is vital in today's fast-changing workplaces. According to Gartner's research in 2021, 'Employees with high trust have 2.6 times the capacity to absorb change.'

As a trustworthy leader, people will find you believable and easy to relate to. In my work, I coach people on how to become a leader whom people trust for their integrity. In this case, the word integrity does not only mean honesty but also alignment with values.

Agile Leadership Pointers

A trustworthy leader is one who leads with integrity—where his words, thoughts, and actions align.

Think of your values as a compass that guides all the words, thoughts, and actions in your work and life. When you are aligned with your values, your authenticity increases. As you consistently demonstrate how your values guide you, trustworthiness will become part of your brand.

That's why my former colleague's actions erased all the trust we had built earlier—when what she claimed to value (being direct) did not line up with her action (routing her concerns to our boss instead of coming to me directly).

People with whom I work often want to improve their leadership brand. I then ask them to clearly state the brand they want to be associated with. In this exercise, vague or generic words are usually not helpful. So I refer them to my 'Leader of Impact' exercise. You can get this from Leadership Agility Force, a membership site for aspiring agile leaders. Visit https://leaderspeoplelove.com/resources for the 'Leader of Impact' exercise. Below is an excerpt from the exercise. You can find the full version online.

The Leader of Impact Exercise

- What are the three most important values that undergird all actions in your work and life?
- How do you demonstrate your values consistently at work and in life?
- How will you communicate your values through thoughts, words, and deeds?
- How will others describe you when you are not in the room? Write down three adjectives or short phrases.

This is followed by the next step.

1. Identify three to five stakeholders (people who know you well) to describe you using three words/adjectives.
2. After collecting all the words, compare what you received with your ideal.
3. This will help inform you of the gaps in your knowledge and where to begin increasing your alignment between your thoughts, words, and deeds.

In addition to using personal values, you might also be keen to explore other definitions of trust. Here are three for your consideration.

- 'Trust is defined as choosing to risk making something you value vulnerable to another person's actions,' according to Charles Feltman's definition of trust explained in *The Thin Book of Trust* (2008).
- Thirteen behaviours based on character and competence from the book *Speed of Trust* by Stephen Covey (2018):
  o Talk straight
  o Demonstrate respect
  o Create transparency
  o Right wrongs
  o Show loyalty
  o Deliver results
  o Get better
  o Confront reality
  o Clarify expectations
  o Practice accountability
  o Listen first
  o Keep commitments
  o Extend trust
- Seven elements of the anatomy of trust are 'Boundaries, Reliability, Accountability, Vault, Integrity, Nonjudgement, and Generosity,' according to Brene Brown's research (2021).

These three definitions are all-encompassing and fairly comprehensive. They may also be used to determine if someone is trustworthy. Whichever you eventually choose as your guide, use it well and consistently, because trust is of utmost importance for organizational leaders.

After the unpleasant incident, my colleague and I continued to work together for a while. However, I became fearful and suspicious of her without the trust in our relationship, despite the superficial harmony. It made me paranoid. I often second-guessed myself with thoughts like, 'Does she really agree with our way forward? What other objectives does she have? Maybe I need to reconfirm with her once more?' Working with her started feeling highly unsafe as I could not trust her words or behaviour. I felt like I had to watch my back constantly, which eventually became too much. My mental health and performance took a hit.

Trust takes more effort to build and precious little to break, so act wisely. Make trustworthiness part of your brand and a guiding principle.

Agile Leadership Pointers

Trust is the antidote for suspicion and ill will. It's the necessary lubricant for difficult conversations, productive conflict, and bridging differences.

8.3. The Courage for Direct Communication

Years ago, as a newly initiated entrepreneur in the coaching and consulting business, I had a hard time finding my way. I have witnessed many purpose-driven coaches venture into the hostile world of business, and have also seen quite a few wind up their business within a short few years as they could not figure out a way to turn coaching into a thriving business.

I was a newborn in this domain and relatively naïve. Sometimes, I had absolutely no idea how to move forward. But my desperation to succeed caused me to turn to unusually bold moves. Desperate times call for desperate measures.

Completely against my reserved, introverted and usually timid nature, I knocked on many established coaches' doors, knowing I would be rejected or humiliated, more often than not. My goal—get a coaching job from them, observe the masters at work and hopefully, learn the ropes for building a thriving business in professional training and coaching myself.

One day, I managed to get an audience with a very established master coach in Singapore. Without going into too much detail—what I learned from this master coach changed the way I approached my practice and business philosophy.

'A lot of coaches serve with a good heart and the intention to help, but Chuen Chuen, do you know what is the one thing that stands in their way of becoming an outstanding coach, and makes that difference in their business?' I was asked. Of course, I did not know the answer but I tried to look thoughtful and smart as I held my breath.

'It is to communicate directly.'

For context, direct communication is one of the core competencies for professional coaches. To be honest, I did not think much of it at first. The master coach explained further.

'You see, what the coachees need is for their coaches to serve as mirrors and reflect what we are picking up. They cannot see it for themselves; that's why we are valuable. People don't dare to tell them the truth. That's why they come to us. But saying what we have observed and reflecting it back truthfully is not always easy. We too have many misgivings: "will the coachee be angered, offended or hurt?" These fears are completely normal. Coaches are humans and yearn to be accepted too. That is why this is the one competency that people struggle to become good at, or tend to develop last because it's also the most difficult and uncomfortable.'

That was honestly the best business and coaching lesson I have ever received.

We eventually went our separate ways and I never got to work with the master coach. But this lesson was firmly etched in my mind, shaping my work and how I show up. Consequently, it also influences the people with whom I interact.

In the business context, direct communication is difficult and challenging because if we need to say something confrontational, it can threaten to tear our professional relationships apart. It gets more complicated when there are competing interests or power differences. We value relationships and goodwill, especially when close collaboration is needed. But some things are too important to not be addressed directly.

I have, however, also met many people who call themselves direct communicators. They have no qualms about calling a spade a spade, but in the process, they damage relationships and goodwill, leaving a trail of burnt bridges in their wake. This is not direct communication but rather, being blunt. It may also be seen as 'obnoxious aggression', as explained in *Radical Candor* (2019) by Kim Scott.

Leaders need to hone their ability to communicate directly while being diplomatic. When it comes to the crunch, it takes guts to share what is on your mind. Speaking up may feel difficult, psychologically, and socially threatening, but it's worthwhile (Smith et al 2019).

To become comfortable with direct communication that's constructive and helpful for the receiver, requires us to first build and then deepen trust.

Key Points in a Snapshot

- A psychologically safe environment is especially necessary for neurodiverse workplaces.
- If unexpected or 'stupid' questions are met with harsh criticism, then very soon, no one except the manager will be speaking.
- Trust is the foundation of a psychologically safe workplace where people can speak up directly; it needs to be part of every leader's brand.

Self-Evaluation

- How do you usually navigate conflicts and disagreements?
- When you feel strongly about something and are the minority holding this view, how do you usually deal with it?
- How directly do you communicate what you truly think and feel?
- Given a choice, would you want to be more direct or less? Why?
- What conditions need to be present for you to feel safe enough to speak your mind?
- How can you then create the conditions incrementally over time, so you will speak up when the time calls for it?

Refer to https://leaderspeoplelove.com/resources
for more resources to increase your agility.

Your Reflections

How do you usually navigate conflicts and disagreements?
When you feel strongly about something and are the minority holding this view, how do you usually deal with it?
How directly do you communicate what you truly think and feel?
Given a choice, would you want to be more direct or less? Why?
What conditions need to be present for you to feel safe enough to speak your mind?
How can you then create the conditions incrementally over time, so you will speak up when the time calls for it?

9

Meet Daniel

A Senior Executive in the Fast-Moving Technology Space, Doubtful about His Value-Add

I can readily recall my first conversation with Daniel. I was looking forward to our session together, intrigued by his cool-sounding title. Though Daniel was outfield that day, he did his best to find a quiet place for our call, showed up and apologized earnestly for not having his video on. Even on a voice call, I was able to get a good idea of who Daniel was, as a person: sincere, responsible, down-to-earth. There was a charismatic quality in Daniel's voice. I was awestruck.

'How nice it would be if he were my manager! His team must be so happy to work with him!' I thought to myself. That was why what he said later surprised me so much that till today, many years since that first conversation, it's still fresh in my mind, as if it had happened just yesterday.

Daniel had been demonstrating outstanding value as a technology leader in his career. He believed he was valued for his ability to give sound advice specific to technology, point out blind spots and help people see connections. To his mind, a leader added value by being the guru—no two ways about it.

During that first call, Daniel shared that he had been thinking about stepping down. Feeling like a fish out of water, he had been tasked to expand his scope and oversee the technology branch, guiding developments in over six highly specialized areas. Many of the engineers and researchers on his team were more knowledgeable than he was, and he was feeling increasingly out of his depth. To make matters worse, feeling vulnerable and exposed agitated him. He struggled to keep a lid on his temper—a façade for his vulnerability—and regulate the strong waves of anger, especially when he felt attacked. Team relationships rapidly deteriorated, with some discussions escalating into shouting matches. After every outburst, Daniel was consumed by guilt for appearing emotional and unprofessional.

Things had become so bad that people were avoiding him in the corridor. Daniel felt rejected, unappreciated and stuck. From his voice alone, the despair was clear.

My work with Daniel centred around helping him redefine what success looks like and then planning strategies for future engagements with his team. Daniel was a different type of leader in his arena and needed to first appreciate his difference as an advantage, to be then able to use that difference to make a significant impact.

10

Theme III: Creating Human-Centred Workplaces

'Emotional intelligence is the ability to recognize and understand emotions in yourself and others, and your ability to use this awareness to manage your behaviour and relationships.'

Travis Bradberry, *Emotional Intelligence 2.0*

What quality do people think leaders need the most in today's workplace?

Empathy—not only according to popular demand, but also research.

A study of 889 employees conducted by Catalyst (Bommel 2021) found empathy in their leaders positively associated with many areas:

- 61 per cent of employees feel more innovative
- 76 per cent feel engaged at work
- 57–62 per cent of women said they are unlikely to leave the organization

- 50 per cent feel their workplace is inclusive
- 86 per cent find themselves juggling work-life demands better

From the Leaders People Love Global Survey, the two empathy-related competencies also emerged at the top. When asked what competencies managers need to lead effectively in disruptive times:

- 78.7 per cent of respondents wanted managers to 'be realistic about challenges on the ground';
- 77.5 per cent of respondents wanted managers to 'lead with empathy'.

Great leaders make great workplaces when they employ a mix of hard and soft skills to create the necessary conditions for optimal performance—happy employees perform better, are more engaged and stay longer in their jobs. To achieve the best organizational performance, empathy is essential for any leader people would love.

To become a leader people love, you need to first bring your whole person into the workplace, and that includes your emotions.

To be comfortable with other people's emotions, first be comfortable with your own.

10.1. Emotions are Natural Aspects of the Human Experience

How would you rate the emotional quality of your workplace?
What kind of emotions are often displayed?
What types of emotions are permitted?
When you think about the word 'emotional', what comes to mind? A hysterical person? Or one who is angry?
What might you be tempted to say to this emotional person? Could it be 'Stop it. This is not the time to be emotional. Let's be logical here'?

Workplace civility is important and we most certainly don't wish to promote aggressive behaviour. We should not, however, ignore the fact that every person experiences negative emotions at times.

We need to watch out for the labels we give the emotions we experience in response to the stimulus around us, and not chide ourselves for being 'bad', 'unprofessional', or 'unworthy'. In workplaces that only permit positive emotions, we might find something called toxic positivity or extreme positivity, where people feel pressured to exhibit only positive emotions and avoid uncomfortable ones.

According to US psychotherapist Amy Morin (2020), a culture of extreme positivity can be damaging, for it can lead to reduced motivation, unpreparedness (since the positivity paints an unrealistic picture), minimizing threats and then reducing one's attention on those areas. It may also cause depression due to the suppression of one's emotions.

Negative emotions are part and parcel of the human experience. They are as natural and undeniable as night and day, life and death, beginning and end. For leaders to navigate the ups and downs that naturally accompany perpetually volatile, uncertain, complex, and ambiguous business contexts, building an emotional capacity and holding space for *both* positive and negative emotions is vital. A workplace can be filled with happy individuals, or be a hotspot for artificial happiness. It takes a wise leader to see the truth and do something about it when needed.

10.2. Emotions Are Helpful Indicators

'I am an emotional leader,' Daniel lamented, 'that's why I'm not fit to lead. I don't deserve this position.'

I felt sad about what society, systems, and cultures had done to Daniel and many others I know. Since when was it wrong to be human? Understandably, Daniel was facing a lot of pressure as a male authority figure, laden with expectations and invisible yardsticks against which he had to measure up. Female leaders may also be constrained by stereotypes (for instance, that they are emotional, soft, and weak), so they too may feel the need to suppress their emotions.

Once, I received some bad news while in the office. The floodgates of my tears dangerously close to bursting, I hastily excused myself from a meeting, escaped to the washroom, slammed the door shut for some privacy, and cried in anguish and shame. As if feeling upset about the bad news was not bad enough, I was also overwhelmed by feelings of inadequacy for being emotional at the workplace. Although I had broken down privately, the rushed exit from the office had laid my emotional side bare for all to witness. I berated myself.

Why am I so weak and cry easily?

Why do I feel so much?

Why can't I be logical?

What will others think of me?

They must be gossiping about me in the meeting room now. I'm so terrible.

Navigating Daniel's Conundrum

When Daniel's voice was dripping with disdain, contempt and disapproval for himself for being 'emotional', I did not contest his point of view as that would not be helpful. Instead, I offered him these questions to evaluate the benefit and harm of emotions, as well as the shifts he wanted to see in himself:

- What did the strong emotions mean?
- What differentiates good emotions from bad ones?
- How can emotions be turned into a force for good instead of a force of destruction?

Daniel took these back as homework and fodder for thought. At the next session, something shifted when Daniel realized some truths about himself.

His strong, visceral emotions indicated that he cared deeply or regarded something highly important. Founded on a core belief about how work should be done, or how he should contribute, his anger and helplessness surged when he felt unable to fulfil his role. The more he tried to deny or suppress the emotions, the more they intensified. The combative persona Daniel gradually constructed, together with the obvious technical gaps he exhibited, increased the team's dislike and animosity towards him. Every time he lost control, it reinforced this negative impression of him.

In truth, his emotions were founded on something positive. This realization helped Daniel normalize how he saw his emotions. The biggest takeaway for him was that his feelings meant he cared.

Agile Leadership Pointers

Emotions can be good or bad depending on how we label them. It's all a matter of perception.

As Daniel effectively de-labelled what it meant to be an emotional leader, we explored a few actionable strategies for him to defuse the tension in the moment and quickly move the discussion towards resolution.

Here are the two powerful strategies Daniel and I worked on:

1. Help people understand the intentions behind the display of emotions. This was especially effective as it helped people understand why he was upset about something, instead of letting them imagine the worst about his character.
2. Redirect the strong 'negative' emotion to drive positive outcomes. When Daniel felt annoyed that the team was not progressing in their project, he could contextualize the emotion and drive them toward action, instead of lashing out.

To help him put these strategies into action, I offered some ways he could respond. Here are the examples I used:

- 'I'm annoyed that the project is delayed because I believe we got the right people on this team, and I trust all your abilities. Let's evaluate what we can do now to meet the deadline.'
- 'I'm feeling angry that you did not alert me about the major incident until now because I believe you have good judgement. I also believe I might have a part to play, and let's see how we can resolve this issue before it gets bigger.'
- 'I'm disappointed that we cannot see eye to eye on this matter yet because I believe we all want the same thing, and the best for our teams. Let's explore how we can understand each other's point of view better now.'

After applying the strategies for a few weeks, things began to change. His teams of engineers became more open and receptive to what he had to say, once his argument sounded a lot less like blame or red-hot anger. People feared him less and their conversations became more vibrant. For Daniel, articulating his feelings and the why, bought him a few precious seconds to recover his composure and remain professional. Feeling more accepted and understood, Daniel became a lot more effective as a leader.

To feel is human. Emotions are natural for any human being.

Self-Evaluation

- What do your strong emotions say about you as a person?
- What makes emotions 'bad'?
- What is the real cause of the supposedly 'bad' emotions?
- How would you change your response and shift the outcomes as you experience strong and negative emotions?

Your Reflections

What do your strong emotions say about you as a person?
What makes emotions 'bad'?
What is the real cause of the supposedly 'bad' emotions?
How would you change your response and shift the outcomes as you experience strong and negative emotions?

10.3. Leading with Vulnerability

'This thing has been on my mind. It's bugging me so much that I don't sleep well on some days. So my team would come to me to "seek direction" but honestly, I don't know this technology as much as they do. I feel like a fraud, and maybe I am. There are so many areas to look into. How will I find time to learn all of them? If I'm completely honest, even if I spend the time, I don't think I can be better than my engineers!' Daniel said, heaving a loud sigh.

'If you are the smartest cookie in the room, then you are in the wrong room.'

An excerpt from Episode 7, *Agile Leaders Conversations* with
Christian Kastner, Sales Director, Germany

Stress levels from work have been on the rise (Gallup Inc. 2023), especially among middle managers. Gallup has found that middle managers are the most highly stressed group, with 35 per cent suffering from burnout (Harter 2021). I too have observed, while supporting leaders since the early days of COVID-19, that more leaders are coming to our sessions feeling overwhelmed and mentally cluttered. That did not surprise me, as poor mental health seems to be correlated with the increased rate of change and disruption organizations are experiencing.

In the Leaders People Love Global Survey, nearly 61.8 per cent of respondents rated the level of disruption they face in their jobs as 'very high' and 62 per cent of respondents rated their managers as navigating changes effectively, out of which only 27.6 per cent rated their managers as 'very effective'. The gap in manager readiness to continuously navigate complexities and uncertainties is clear. To break out of the vicious cycle, managers need to calibrate their self-expectations and support themselves better.

That's why leading with vulnerability is an important idea for leaders to consider today.

Leading with vulnerability is not new. Made popular first by Brene Brown's 2018 bestseller, *Dare to Lead*, how to lead with vulnerability has been one of the most commonly raised topics of discussion in my work with leaders from all over the world. In the past, leaders could continue to lead by instructing, directing, and being the 'smartest cookie in the room', but it's becoming increasingly unwise to do so.

The questions they often ask are:

- How can one feel confident even when they are also new to the situation and are figuring things out like everybody else?
- How can one keep a cool head when changes are endless?
- How can one remain calm when old methods no longer work and new solutions are nowhere in sight?
- How best to deal with so many moving parts?

No One Has All the Answers

Frequently, leaders will encounter situations where they feel vulnerable or even incapable because they don't have the answer. In fact, we might have to accept the truth that nobody has all the answers. Magic potions and secret formulas don't exist. So instead of holding ourselves to impossible standards or trying to be the 'smartest cookie' in the room or the one with the answers, leaders need to learn to lead with vulnerability. In a world where it's impossible to have all the answers, it's wiser to develop the ability to make decisions even when limited answers are available.

Leading with vulnerability is not a nice-to-have, but rather, a must-have strategy. Many of you will feel increasingly vulnerable. Normalizing how you see vulnerability or saying, 'I don't have the answer yet', will increase resilience and protect your mental health, and that of your teams and organizations.

Navigating Daniel's conundrum

For Daniel, we returned to one of the first questions I had posed to him: In spite of his deep knowledge in only one domain, why was he promoted and tasked to look after the six technology areas? His answer: He had a knack for fostering collaboration and integration within the organization.

Over the years, he had been highly effective as the interface between his team and senior management. His team members could appreciate the connection between the work they did and the larger purpose. As a result, engagement from his team was always high and their results, stellar. When engaging the senior management, he was always able to clearly articulate the team's value and future aspirations, garnering support and resources to embark on more futuristic and revolutionary work, creating a productive cycle of value creation and results.

In other words, Daniel was promoted for his ability to be an effective bridge between the layers and units of the organization, and much less for his technical expertise.

Agile Leadership Pointers

The ability to connect the pieces and facilitate seamless collaboration is especially valuable in a diverse and divided world.

For Daniel, now having recognized the true value he brought to the table, which had not eroded but been enhanced by his involvement in the six technology areas, he was ready to lead with courageous vulnerability.

Perspectives on Vulnerability

For leaders reading this, I wish to offer some alternative perspectives.

- It's okay to not know everything. What's not okay is not knowing and pretending to know, or refusing to find out.
- If you don't know, ask. If you don't ask, you'll never know.
- You need discernment to recognize if the environment is safe enough for you to be vulnerable. When it's not safe to ask questions at your workplace, seek support elsewhere so you can figure it out.
- Even if you don't know the details (let the experts handle it), you'll be able to add value conceptually. Technology, like many

other domains, is built on high-level concepts that will remain true for a long time.

- Your greatest value-add eventually might not be knowing the answers per se, but asking high-value questions that lead to stellar results. To help people focus their energies, ask questions at the conceptual and abstract levels, instead of getting lost in the weeds of minutiae. Elevate yourself and your team's thinking by asking better questions.

Agile Leadership Pointers

Multiply the collective potential of your team, not diminish it with your ego.

Caution

Here are some words of caution to keep in mind so you can reap the most benefits from leading with vulnerability:

- If you find yourself often in a position of 'I don't know the answer', ask yourself, 'what do I *need* to know?' Knowledge gaps are the easiest to fill, so act on those quickly and don't let the issue fester.
- Leading with vulnerability does not mean sharing everything without filters. Consider the risks and implications that could arise as a result of your sharing, or oversharing.
- In conversations where the solution is unclear, turn it into a learning opportunity. For example, you might share your decision-making process. It may sound something like 'I cannot make a decision about this yet, but if I know A, B, C, and D, then I'll be able to better figure things out. How can we figure out A, B, C, and D, so we can collectively make a sound decision?'

10.4. Treat Yourself Right

In January 2023, Prime Minister of New Zealand Jacinda Arden announced her resignation. Without going into details about her work as a politician, as an advocate for neurodiversity among leaders, Jacinda

Arden was undeniably recognized as a role model for leaders—kind and strong.

In her resignation speech, a few key ideas stood out:

- There is time to give your all, for as long as you can.
- After that time, when you cannot give anymore, it's best to step away.
- You can be your own kind of leader—one who knows when it's time to go.

In sharing this, I am not encouraging you to leave whatever you are doing, but simply reminding you that when the seasons change, where and how you contribute can change, too. When the time for engaging effectively in something ends, it's time to move on to something else, because something better is waiting for your contribution.

View your leadership and career as a journey. At different times in your life, you will need different things. Many leaders I know are self-sacrificial and push themselves too far. However, beware of the last straw that breaks the camel's back—some damages are not easily reversible.

Good leaders are rare. They must take care of themselves so their leadership journey can enjoy longevity, and their contributions can be long-lasting and satisfying.

This was something both Jane and Daniel paid heed to. Instead of relentlessly pushing forward, they stepped back and re-evaluated where and how they contribute. Learning to cut themselves some slack renewed their motivation and energy, and their results shifted.

Key Points in a Snapshot

- Emotions are normal for all members of the workplace, and can be skilfully directed to achieve positive outcomes.
- Strong emotions indicate that one cares deeply about an issue.
- It's becoming increasingly difficult for leaders to have all the answers in the current business climate so you need another operating model.
- Instead of expecting one person to know everything, it's more useful to learn to leverage all the experts in the ecosystem.
- A leader who is burnt out is not good for anyone, so take care of yourself.

11

Outcomes for Jane and Daniel

With Jane and Daniel, we worked on the themes related to the Captain.

For Jane, it was to redefine what it meant to be a leader, discover hidden assumptions that influenced her behaviour which, in turn, shaped her team's interactions with her. For Daniel, it was to normalize feelings and emotions and redirect the strong emotions for constructive purposes.

Both Jane and Daniel also had to uncover why they were tasked to lead, in what ways they added value, and how to extract themselves from the limiting definition of a leader as the subject-matter expert.

At the end of our work together, these were the results.

11.1. Jane

Jane, after establishing a new way of working with her remaining team members, was able to align how they would support one another.

Coming to a shared agreement reaped many benefits. The open discussion helped them clarify many assumptions and specify how each member hoped to do their work and how they wished to be motivated. Norms were also established around the cadence and sequencing of work, modes and rules of collaboration. Putting down these rules of collaboration was liberating, for Jane now knew exactly when to give her team space and when to swoop in to help.

Over time, as trust was rebuilt, Jane was able to improve her team's performance and increase their individual skills and effectiveness.

Once she stopped micromanaging, Jane started experiencing less stress than before. Once she trusted her team and had the confidence that their goals were aligned, she was able to elevate herself to leading by spending more time studying trends and determining strategy. That raised her to a position of a leader people love, for her team were truly inspired and eager to hear about her visionary strategies.

You may refer to https://leaderspeoplelove.com/resources for the 'Way of Working' document you can use to determine the leadership needs of your team.

11.2. Daniel

My last session with Daniel could not have happened at a better time. It was their annual Staff Appreciation Day, where employees were encouraged to send written cards of appreciation to people who have made a difference in their work.

In the preceding years, Daniel would receive few or no cards at all. That year, after nearly a year of working together to redirect his emotions for good, Daniel walked into his office and was pleasantly surprised. There, on his table, was a huge stack of appreciation cards; it was overflowing—a sharp contrast from the past years. In just a year, Daniel had transformed from being an undesirable emotional leader who people feared meeting in the corridor (and one who people talked about behind his back), into a leader people loved.

One of the cards bore these words: 'You showed me what it means to lead with emotions. Your courage and deep passion inspire me, and working with you has been the best part of my career. Thank you for being my manager. I will continue to do my best!'

Daniel's parting words to me could not have been more perfect: 'I'm an emotional leader—and I'm proud to be one.'

Refer to https://leaderspeoplelove.com/resources
for complete resources and strengthen the captain in you.

THE DEVELOPER

IGNITING THE BEST POTENTIAL IN PEOPLE

Who was the person who shaped you into the leader you are today?

I received this question at a workshop. Upon reflecting at my leadership journey, I realized, with a tinge of sadness, that the number of good leaders who had come into my life were few and far between. If I were to make a proper count, the total would be fewer than the number of fingers on my hand.

My experience might be an outlier. If you were blessed with many great leaders in your career, I'm happy for you. Good leaders shape our lives in unimaginable ways. Their touch lingers on years after we have left the shelter of their wings of guidance. I noticed that the few leaders who have shaped me into the leader I am today share these similarities:

- They always asked the hard questions that made me think better.
- They never forced me to follow their way blindly. Instead, they respected me as an intellectual and gave me choices.
- They allowed me space to develop in my own way, accelerating my growth by recognizing my strengths before I could even see them myself.
- They didn't mince their words when I deserved to hear their feedback. Their kindness made it easier for me to learn the tough lessons.

Great leaders are the firm hands that guide the ignorant and help transform them into wise leaders who would, in turn, nurture more great leaders. I'm glad I had a few significant ones in my life.

12

Why the Developer Is a Leader People Love

The Developer sees deep meaning in nurturing others' growth. Driven by a personal need to continuously learn, grow, and develop, the Developer also genuinely wants to help others succeed. In the Agile Leadership Superpower Quiz, the Developer is also one of the most common ways in which the leaders we surveyed lead, with 24.1 per cent of over 3,200 leaders leading with this inner voice.

They are good teachers who use coaching skills appropriately to help others think and perform better. Younger employees who prize growth and development in their careers will value the Developer and the opportunity to grow under their leadership.

The Developer is also an effective facilitator who leads generative and inclusive conversations while skilfully enhancing the psychological safety needed to encourage innovation and healthy risk-taking. Active listening, empathy, humility, and critical thinking are essential skills for the Developer.

Refer to https://leaderspeoplelove.com/resources
for more tools and strategies.

13

Inside the Hearts of Bad Bosses
Is a Misguided Developer

Who is a bad boss in your opinion? What did this person do to make you feel that he is bad?

Was it rude and transactional behaviour?

Was he dismissive when you made a genuine mistake?

Did he say insensitive things like 'don't make your problem my problem' or 'come to me with solutions, not problems'?

Many years ago, I worked with Sam, a data scientist who was having a lot of issues with his immediate supervisor. Anticipating a meeting with her would leave him in shreds, worrying and fretting about what nasty things she might have to say to him. To him, she was the most inconsiderate, insensitive, and unkind person on the face of the planet whose sole purpose in life was to make someone's life—his life—miserable.

'I'm doing my best to do my job! Why is she intentionally making my life so difficult?!' he exclaimed exasperatedly.

I can understand his frustration. Years ago, I too had a very tough boss. Whenever I had to go to his office to get approval on a project,

I would get ridiculously anxious and run to the toilet multiple times to compose myself. Just the thought of hearing his harsh words of criticism triggered a stress response in my body that lingered for days after. My throat would tighten and my breathing would turn shallow. To my horror and disgust, my voice would sound squeaky. My hands would tremble involuntarily and my ears redden with shame when he pointedly criticized the gaps in my thinking or the weaknesses of my work. Sometimes, I did not even last ten seconds before he managed to totally, unreservedly deflate my well-conceived plans. For context, my meetings with this tough boss were mostly one-on-one, so the only injury I sustained was a bruised ego.

Most of us value recognition and wish to be seen in a positive light, so situations in which we attract cold blades of criticism or harsh words of disapproval wound our spirits. After each interaction with this boss, I died a little inside. I did not enjoy working with him at all and he was certainly not a leader I loved working with.

But one day, everything changed.

I bumped into him once while I was doing my weekly marketing rounds. There he was—the worst boss on earth! From a distance, I spotted him walking patiently behind his aged parent, holding her hand with great gentleness as she shuffled her feet at a painfully slow pace toward the market. In contrast to the harsh frown lines that would crease his forehead when he looked at my 'substandard' work, he had a gentle look of calm and kindness on his face then.

Just as it dawned on me that this bad boss who seemed to enjoy making my life miserable was also a kind and patient son, he happened to notice me. To my utter surprise, he raised his hand and waved with a smile. I had no choice but to approach.

'Ma, this is Chuen Chuen, the dynamic and smart colleague I have been telling you about,' my bad boss said as he introduced me to his mother.

That one interaction changed everything. I realized I had been dehumanizing him in my mind, making him a villain. The accumulation of our unpleasant interactions had clouded my judgement and tipped the scales against him in my mind. I had forgotten to be objective and fair to him at a human level.

The next day, when I went to the office, I had to again get his approval on a proposal. After shaking off the usual nerves, this time I decided to take a different approach. I shared with him how surprised I was that he introduced me as his 'dynamic and smart colleague' to his mother.

He said, 'Yeah, that's what I always think of you. You didn't crack under pressure, answered my tough questions well and improved each time. When I raised the bar, you rose to the challenge. This was the kind of training I did not get when I was younger, as my manager left me alone to figure things out. Fumbling around in the dark was very stressful and frustrating for me. I also lost a lot of learning opportunities at the time. That's why when I became a manager, I told myself I must teach all of you everything I know. That means not letting people off the hook too easily because tough training is the best training. You have done well so far and I'm proud.'

Hearing this rare and once-in-a-lifetime praise, my ears turned red. This time, it was not because I felt humiliated, but because I had passed an unfair judgement about who my boss was as a person. His tough questions and harsh attitude were not a manifestation of a bad personality. He had been doing what he felt was right and helpful, based on his experience and to the best of his ability. He was a Developer, albeit misguided.

At my core, I believe people are good by nature. In the hearts of bad bosses, I believe, lie good intentions. Hidden behind actions that make us feel uncomfortable and unappreciated is a heart that wants to help people learn and add value to their lives. There's a Developer in them too.

In a personal capacity, I have also worked with senior leaders sent to be coached for their abrasive behaviours that had driven staff out the door. They often defended themselves thus:

- 'I must scold them and make them learn! Look! They did improve leaps and bounds when I did, right? And then instead of appreciating and thanking me, they gave me bad feedback!'
- 'People must be scolded to learn. That's what worked for me.'

- 'Some of these people make the same mistakes repeatedly. Of course, I have to be harsh on them! How else are they going to lead others in future?!'
- 'That was how my boss trained us to be tough and sharp. What's wrong with this method?'

I had hoped to help Sam possibly see a different side of his bad boss. So I asked him, 'From what you described, I think it could be that your boss intends to try and help you. Honestly, in my years of working with people, I have never met anyone who would twiddle their thumbs while drinking coffee after breakfast, thinking, "Now . . . whose day shall I mess up today?" What comes to mind when I say this?'

Sam paused, chuckled a little at the ridiculous mental image, and responded with more lightness: 'Nah . . . she's not a bad person . . . You are right. Her behaviour and questions make her hard to get along with, that's all. It would be healthier for me to take a step back, look at things from her perspective and try to understand where she is coming from.'

I believe many of you have had experiences with bad bosses. If you are working with one now, try your best to look beyond their behaviour. Some of them have been guided by equally harsh and ineffective methods, so those are, unfortunately, the only methods they know to utilize as managers. With limited perspectives and tools, they are restricted by what they know. Many are simply doing what they think is best in the ways they know how, because no one has shown them a better way.

There is, of course, no reason to tolerate bad behaviour. You still want to deal with them constructively. I am confident, however, that you will be different from them.

Now, having been exposed to a different way to guide others, you can deploy more effective methods to engage your team and deliver great work. You have a better chance of helping others achieve their fullest potential and making the experience more positive. As you hone this skill and mindset of becoming a Developer, your road will be different—with this voice, you will become a better manager, and more importantly than that, you will pave the way that inspires more people to become leaders people love.

Key Points in a Snapshot

- Most people lead the way they were led; teach the way they were taught. While role modelling is a powerful tool, leaders must recognize that past models (scripts) might no longer be relevant. People who repeatedly rely on outdated methods might be referred to as 'bad bosses'.
- To increase your relevance and effectiveness as a leader, you need to broaden your perspectives and expand your toolkit.

14

Ensure People Stay Employable to Address Talent Crunch

Meiling, a senior director, shared with me some alarming statistics from a pulse survey conducted by her organization. Employees were asked to rate their confidence level about whether or not they felt like they had relevant skills to remain employable in the next three years, to which a whopping 50 per cent responded they were 'not confident' or 'not very confident'.

Meiling was deeply disturbed as these results indicated that her organization was ineffective in upskilling their employees. This was concerning, especially since her industry was fast-developing, so opportunities to learn, grow, and develop were vast and abundant.

They were seeing limited success at hiring and experienced people were leaving faster than they were being replaced. Vast resources were needed to train a new joiner to become fully independent. Meiling knew something needed to be done about her internal training programmes so they could:

1. meet the organization's needs for expertise and quality;
2. meet employees' needs to feel skilled enough to secure their future.

Some managers may argue that each employee should bear the responsibility to upskill and remain competitive and employable on their own. Depending on your philosophy about human resources, you might also have different views about adding value to your people. You might think, 'What if I train them and they leave?'

'Train people well enough so they can leave, treat them well enough so they don't want to.'

Sir Richard Branson, CEO of The Virgin Group

These concerns are valid and there are no simple answers. However, with the global talent crunch and aging population, organizations can choose between two options:

1. Leverage technology and artificial intelligence to increase the overall effectiveness per human.
2. Regard every person in the organization as an asset who appreciates with your investment, so that they can do better work.

The choice you make would vary based on your industry and job function.

Against the global backdrop, I believe there is strong enough reason for leaders to invest in building internal capabilities by maximizing the potential of every individual in their organization. Imagine everyone on your team is a high-potential and outstanding performer. Beyond ensuring business longevity and profitability, the actions leaders take could shape people's experiences greatly, since people spend most of their waking hours at work. A study conducted in 2019 by Krauss and Orth reports that 'people's self-esteem is influenced by experiencing success or failure in the work domain'—where higher self-esteem improves their social relationships, work experiences, and mental health.

In a nutshell, enabling a culture where people can be successful and productively engaged at work can create more happiness in the world.

Key Points in a Snapshot

- The talent crunch and aging population mean every employee must be maximized to their fullest potential. Leaders play a major role here.
- People's self-esteem rises when they experience greater success at work.

Agile Leadership Pointers

There's a star player in every employee, waiting to be awakened by the right Developer.

15

Meet Alya

A Millennial C-suite Leader Managing a Multi-Generational Team

'I feel like I cannot take my eyes off my people, even for a second. If I so much as squeeze my eyes shut and sneeze for a moment, someone makes a mistake and everything falls apart. Then it's up to me to pick up the pieces and fix the mess again.' Alya heaved exhaustedly, her shoulders drooping with fatigue.

Alya had inherited a multi-generational team with varied competency levels from her long-time predecessor at her company. Having no formal house rules until she came on board, the team had grown accustomed to their previous haphazard way of working. At the same time, Alya struggled to establish processes and streamline operations. Her efforts of bringing in new ways of working—which to her were the norms—were either outrightly resisted or poorly assimilated.

The results? Poor execution, multiple alignment sessions to teach and reteach, low adoption of new tools she had acquired to improve workflow and efficiency supposedly, plus the weariness from the entire exercise was weighing everyone down.

Having received news from her company's management that she would soon be expanding her portfolio to oversee another arm of the business, she knew she had to get her current team up to speed at double the pace and in half the time. We identified a few issues to address early on in our engagement.

As a C-suite leader, Alya did not have adequate talent at the various levels to whom she could rely and delegate work. Over time, job roles may have evolved but people's skill sets have not kept up. Not having the 'right people on the right seat' was taking a toll on her. Alya was effectively covering a few levels of expertise (not so much on a hierarchical level but in terms of offering her subject-matter expertise), which left her little to no time to attend to strategic matters.

Alya had been repeatedly teaching the same skills and problem-solving procedures to her team, but little knowledge was transferred. Her style and expectations were very different from her predecessor's and her team was feeling the strain of that. As they continued to repeat their mistakes, Alya's frustration and annoyance increased, further disrupting the harmony and congeniality in the team as her responses became terse at times. Some team members exhibited a low appetite to upskill and change processes and frequently complained, 'why change it when it's not broken?' or 'my process has been working fine all this time'. Others were a little more adventurous and enthused by new systems, but the gaps in their competencies and low-risk appetites wore Alya down over time.

With her imminent role expansion and declining mental health, we needed to improve her Developer mindset and skills rapidly.

16

Theme IV: Enabling a Culture
of Continuous Learning and Excellence

Enabling a culture of learning in any organization is essential for success. As market conditions continue to be disrupted by emerging technologies, employees need new mindsets and skills to stay relevant and employable. That, coupled with longer life expectancy and shrinking labour force across the world, also means that learning, and staying *trainable and teachable* are necessary for all individuals from all generations, should they continuously yearn for work to be purposeful and enjoyable.

Nurturing a workplace culture where people can learn and grow is paramount. Leaders need to create a safe environment where new ideas and knowledge can be assimilated, creativity fostered, and innovation and growth spurred. In an environment that values education and lifelong development, employees feel supported and motivated to take on challenges. This can lead to increased job satisfaction, increasing loyalty, and enhancing employee retention.

Ultimately, a culture of learning helps create a positive work environment in which everyone is encouraged to strive for excellence.

16.1. The Best Leaders Are Good Teachers

'Your job as a manager is to help people think better, and do better.'

An excerpt from Episode 3, *Agile Leaders Conversations* with
Tang Li Chow, HR Director, Singapore

An article written by Ron Carucci titled 'To Be a Good Manager, You Have to Be a Good Teacher', published by *Harvard Business Review* in 2022, stated, 'It's common for newer leaders to make assumptions about what their team can do, giving assignments without fully vetting whether someone has the skill, knowledge, or experience to succeed.'

Some leaders might contest the proposition that a leader needs to be a good teacher. They may feel that their job is to get the work done and that teaching should not be their job, but that of schools. But given that work is always evolving, the workforce needs to be learning continuously, throughout their lives. Returning to school and taking courses formally is one way to do so. Learning on the job is another— this is where managers come into play. The mindset that people become 'finished products' once formal education is completed is an idea we can no longer afford to have. Insisting on this mindset will create a lot of dissatisfaction and stress for people.

Think instead of formal education as a means of preparation for work and life, and workplaces as an extension of that learning. People are perpetual works-in-progress and managers can play a meaningful role in helping them grow and develop.

You might also think relying on high performers to get the work done is sufficient because 'who has time to teach other people to do their work?' This thinking is also flawed. With the ongoing talent crunch, your high performers are in high demand everywhere. So instead of putting all your eggs in one basket, consider increasing the size of your talent pool by growing more talents. With this in view, how about developing an organization where managers are also the best teachers, so *everyone* can have a chance to become a high performer?

'Experience is not the best teacher. Evaluated experience is. Reflective thinking is needed to turn experience into insight.'

Dr John C. Maxwell

So this was the first task I assigned Alya: to list her team's strengths and weaknesses.

Self-Evaluation

- How well do you know your team's strengths and weaknesses?
- How well do you understand your strengths and weaknesses?
- How can you turn each work task into a meaningful learning experience?
- How can you get the most out of past experiences and maximize learning?

Your Reflections

How well do you know your team's strengths and weaknesses?
How well do you understand your strengths and weaknesses?
How can you turn each work task into a meaningful learning experience?
How can you get the most out of past experiences and maximize learning?

16.2. Teach People to Fish

Years ago, when I first set up home, I did not even know how to cook rice. Up until then, the only times I cooked was during home economics lessons in school. Cooking rice was not in the curriculum, as far as I can remember. It did not help that I was not interested in cooking, so I escaped the kitchen for as long as possible.

Day one after I moved out of my parents' place, I approached some colleagues regarding this business of cooking rice. They were shocked. But from them, I gathered enough information about how to measure the water and rice, that I could manage. Unfortunately, as I rarely cooked, my culinary skills were poor. I had missed all the early opportunities to improve my cooking skills to an acceptable level, so by the time I became an adult, it was too demotivating to even try. Escaping felt far easier.

In Alya's case, too, such a story was unfolding.

Navigating Alya's Conundrum

The many new technological tools she brought in to digitize her team's work overwhelmed them. So feeling helpless and worried, their instinct was to come to Alya—the guru—with their problems whenever they got stuck. But now she was faced with a dilemma. Should she fix the issue for them, give them the solution immediately and move on to another task, or should she coach them until they can perform the task independently?

This is a common issue I have observed in many workplaces. When a subordinate does a piece of work poorly, the manager usually struggles between the following two options:

1. Take over the work completely and relieve them of the responsibility. Doing it yourself is the quickest, most attractive fix, because the clock is always ticking. Better quality of work will be guaranteed and more effortlessly achieved this way. This is the time-driven decision.
2. Guide others through the process, show them how if you need to and let them try again—and potentially make the mistake again. In other words, teach them to fish instead of

delivering the fish to them on a platter. This is the learning-driven decision.

Logically, the managers I work with know option 2 is better in the long run. But over the years, I have met so many leaders who repeatedly chose option 1 out of convenience and time pressure. I can understand that circumstances are not ideal and it does require far more energy and self-restraint to pick option 2. But falling into this trap of convenience consistently ensures that poor results follow, almost always. This is the usual outcome:

- Team members start 'dumbing down'—why should they bother thinking when all of it's already done by the top?
- Teams produce persistently poor-quality work, increasing the manager's workload astronomically—'why get it right when my manager would fix it anyway? All I have to do is apologize' and then the cycle repeats.
- Everything feels critical and overwhelming—often, work is sent for 'approval' at the last minute, leaving the manager little choice but to take over the work. Too often, the manager also needs to do a major overhaul and then submit the work further upward for approval.
- The manager is exposed to increased risk and pressure, increasing stress levels and fear of making mistakes, as fewer people are looking out for any errors and blind spots—'above my pay grade, so not my problem' attitude.
- A poor leadership pipeline is formed when the leader eventually gets stuck as there is no ready successor, or an incompetent manager is promoted to fill the vacancy owing to limited choices.
- High-performing members are either over-stretched and need to take on additional work, or feel that they are not fairly recognized, or leave because they are not cognitively challenged.

The consequences of choosing option 1 consistently, in my experience, are *always* poor. The environment becomes reactive;

everyone feels that they need to scramble to get things done—always in fight-or-flight mode. No wonder then that people feel burnt out and stressed in such an environment. High stress levels leads to poor well-being and with that, everything goes downhill and it turns into a lose-lose situation for all.

I can understand the reality of time pressure and the need for speed. But being in a reactive environment where you are constantly being chased by deadlines is not sustainable in the long run. Imagine always dreaming about work, or hardly getting adequate sleep over long periods.

Alya was beginning to see some of these ill effects of the work environment. She hardly ever dared to go on leave or take sick leave, as she knew how dependent her team was on her. Even when on holiday, she would take her laptop along and guiltily sneak in some hours of work. While she was starting to learn to teach her people to fish, people did struggle. She found it hard to stop rescuing them. We had to first evaluate what steps were possible for her to remedy her situation, one step at a time.

Actions to Consider

The leadership mandate you have is to start teaching people to fish so that they can fish independently of you, eventually. Some actions you can consider to achieve this:

- Instead of giving away the answer too quickly, pause. Ask questions to help them think through issues. Thinking on their behalf doesn't help.
- If time permits, fight the instinct to rescue them or to take over the work. Guide them to work through the issue (that is your investment on human assets) and watch their value appreciate.
- Make a list of the strengths and weaknesses of each team member, along with their interests and career aspirations.
- Assign the right task so it's a stretch task, but not an impossible task. When the difficulty or nature of the task is incorrect, it can either lead to boredom or overwhelm.

- Set up learning partnerships by pairing up members. Learning alone can be frightening.
- Make time to reflect and review project outcomes, whenever possible. Each reflective exercise maximizes the learning and helps people internalize their takeaways.

Agile Leadership Pointers

Set up tasks of incremental difficulty so people can taste success and improve over time.

Getting started is difficult because we are breaking long-standing patterns and habits, but the potential benefits downstream are too precious to not give it a try.

> 'The mediocre teacher tells. The good teacher explains. The superior teacher demonstrates. The great teacher inspires.'
>
> General William Ward

The leader is akin to the teacher. Be a great teacher.

Self-Evaluation

What's your first response when someone makes a mistake? How can you begin to lead with the Developer voice?

Your Reflections

What's your first response when someone makes a mistake? How can you begin to lead with the Developer voice?

16.3. The Issue Isn't with Hearing but with Comprehension

'Listen—It's step 1, step 2, and then step 3, right? Do you understand? You get it now?'

Back in the days, when I was a mathematics teacher, this was something I would utter often. You might find some of these questions familiar as people often bring the same line of questioning into homes, schools, as well as in the workplace.

As an educator, I wanted to help my students understand the world of numbers. Mathematics was relatively easy for me; I found it a breeze. I thought all I had to do was to share my thinking process with my students. So each day, I would go to class, pick mathematical problems apart, show my students how I would look at each problem, show them my steps as I tackled it, and voilà! A beautiful solution would emerge.

There was an insider joke about QED or *quod erat demonstrandum*, meaning 'which was to be demonstrated'. Those of us who found the subject simple would joke that QED should be renamed 'quite easily done' because, 'Look! With my steps 1, 2, and 3—there it is! The answer! As easy as 1, 2, 3!'

But the reality is, not everyone could follow my train of thought. This is why understanding neurodiversity is so important for leaders—everybody's brain works differently.

Those naturally inclined towards the subject saw mathematics as 'one of the most beautiful languages in the world', while others saw it as the bane of their existence and a source of misery. As a young teacher, I wanted to help all my charges appreciate the subject as much as possible, so they could do well at their yearly examinations.

After-school remedials were offered to students who struggled with the subject. This is not unlike the follow-up meeting you would call once you realize, with some level of horror or confusion, that some who were physically present in the meeting did not reach the same level of mental understanding about the way forward as others.

At these remedials, I would say, 'See—It's step 1, step 2, and then step 3. Right? Do you understand? You get it now?' Some students would get it this time, but some still would not.

At the next remedial, I'd repeat each word slower, louder, and frustration dripping from my tone of voice: 'Seeeee—It's steeeep 1, steeeeep 2, and then steeeeep 3. RIGHT? Do you UNDERSTAND? You GET IT noowwww?'

Do you see the mistake I made? I repeated the same instructions in exactly the same way as before, as if they had not heard me the first time. I also repeated myself slower and louder (from frustration, mainly) each subsequent time as if hearing the same thing again would help them understand better. All that I accomplished from this was demotivating my students as I openly expressed my helplessness and frustration at their 'incompetence'. As expected, this way of conducting after-school remedials was a classic example of how 'high effort, low results' played out.

That's not all. I was also often tired and stretched because of the extra hours I had to put in, repeating what had been taught before, with little to show for the additional effort. I, too, was discouraged.

Sadly, I had few alternatives to learn from. Without better role models, my colleagues at that time and I honestly did not know better. It was only some years later as I attended professional development workshops for educators that I realized my mistake. That's why everyone—leaders, teachers, experts, professionals—needs to continuously upgrade and expand their skill set.

When someone cannot (or would not) follow your line of thinking, the issue is not with their hearing but their understanding. It's also not pure stubbornness or their refusal to acknowledge your point of view. Getting angry or impatient with them is not going to help. Often, their lack of understanding is because:

- Something is not making sense to them, or
- It's conflicting with their belief.

These are the real issues you need to address using your Developer skills.

Building Blocks

So how we as leaders need to tackle the issue, is by first assessing what the other person does understand. Think of learning as building blocks. You need to lay the first layer, then the second, and so forth. Too often, we impatiently want to get to the top layer without building the bottom foundation.

Knowledge is constructed when people have the blocks
they can add on to prior experience and knowledge.

As I shared with Alya about my mistake as a young teacher, she began to understand what she needed to change. Instead of repeating the same instructions or teaching in the same way as before, she decided to try one of the following:

1. Ask questions so you can find out what made sense or what did not make sense to your team members in the first instance.
2. Explain in a different way. For example, use stories, analogies, or metaphors.
3. Ask someone to explain it using their own words.
4. When it's not a matter of (logical) understanding, figure out what is the real concern (emotional/belief).

You might notice the steps above are all others-oriented instead of self-oriented. That's also a quality that all leaders today need—empathy. To be empathetic is simply to see the world through the eyes of others, understand how they make decisions, and then make sense of the world. Having empathy will help you influence, persuade, and upskill people more effectively.

Agile Leadership Pointers

To help others understand your world, you first need to understand theirs.

16.4. Better Questions Beget Better Responses

Leveraging coaching style as a leadership style is not a new idea. Many coachees I have worked with have attended coaching skills workshops prior to working with me. Depending on how the programme was structured and executed, some of them might have started applying coaching skills in daily work conversations, while others may have regarded it as mere theories for an ideal world, inapplicable to their reality.

Based on anecdotal input, it appears to me that many leaders have not personally experienced the benefits of coaching style. When asked, they could hardly name anyone who used the style effectively to elevate the quality of thinking and accelerate learning, while preserving psychological safety and evoking creativity and resourcefulness.

Those who had a good experience and were effectively coached by their managers, always referred to it as the golden period of exponential growth and deep satisfaction, as their self-awareness also increased massively. Good leadership is almost always built from 'borrowed insights' and deep personal mastery, so coaching skills are certainly important and many leaders would certainly benefit from learning them.

In this section, I will address a few commonly held misconceptions about the coaching style for managers and offer actionable tips you can use to draw out the best potential of your people by leading with a coach's mindset and then asking better questions that accelerate growth and maturity.

Misconception 1: The Manager as a Coach Simply Asks Questions

This common misconception results from an over-generalization that equates coaching with simply asking questions. Applying this, managers may mistakenly turn every instruction into a question.

Between telling, instructing, and asking questions, one generally prefers that managers first ask questions and then offer answers. The rationale is that we want to nurture an environment where people can think independently before coming to the manager for solutions. Encouraging people to think or form their own opinions before giving them the answer will help increase their capacity and also lighten the manager's workload.

However, when this idea of 'simply turning instructions into questions' results in questions like the following . . .

- Why didn't you do A?
- Why didn't you think of B?
- Why not C?
- Did you think of D?
- Have you spoken to person E?
- Can you do F instead?

(A sidenote: The tone of the questioner also plays a part in their effectiveness.)

These kind of questions are problematic as they are either close-ended or leading questions with a single 'correct answer' in mind. When you expect a solution and are constantly evaluating the 'correctness' of the other person's responses, these become poor questions that generate low-quality results.

When you get a lousy answer, check the quality of your questions.

Then, what is the coaching style and what do good questions look like?

Asking better questions

Fundamentally, leading with a coach's mindset means that you:

- Have unconditional positive regard for the other person;
- Believe that the person is resourceful and able to find solutions;
- Let go of what you believe is right (there's space to do that, as you will find out in the next section).

To be more effective at asking questions, three criteria need to be met:

1. Withhold judgement about what the right answer looks like.
2. Questions need to expand thinking or broaden perspectives, and help uncover thinking patterns, assumptions, or connections not seen previously.
3. Converge to a resolution or decision only after thoroughly understanding the issue.

Agile Leadership Pointers

Good questions expand thinking or broaden perspectives before converging to resolutions, decisions, or actions. Poor ones limit your results.

Using the criteria above, the questions above would be more effective if they were rephrased as:

- What is your assessment about A?
- B might be promising. What are your thoughts?
- What would make C a possibility?
- What else do we need to think about?
- Who else do we need to speak with to get more insight?
- What other opportunities are available for our consideration?

Many managers struggle to turn closed questions into open questions because as managers, they often have a preferred approach or a clearer view of what would work. This is natural and understandable. That's why the next misconception is important for managers who want to lead as coaches effectively.

Misconception 2: Leading with a Coaching Style Means I Musn't Share What I Think

Managers need to first understand that coaching as a leadership style is not the same as being a professional coach. A formal coaching relationship is one of equal power, meaning both the coach and coachee are partners and equals. This first premise is already not met in a manager–employee relationship.

The relationship between a manager and an employee is often naturally unequal because one person is directly responsible for the team's results, and the performance of one depends on the other. In such a relationship, the manager naturally has more power than the employee. This is why coaching principles cannot be applied universally when managers lead with a coaching style.

In a professional coaching relationship, the coach might share his or her thinking after asking for permission. But in a manager–employee relationship, you might not need to do that.

Even when you know a possible solution, however, there are benefits if you can share your thinking without imposing your views. Reconsider how and when you share your opinion, to avoid a situation where people 'guess what the top wants' or 'answer the test' instead of brainstorming and thinking from a fresh perspective, or are motivated to get a quick decision from the decision-maker so as to move things along without applying themselves.

Sharing your solution too early might also give rise to group thinking, where everyone aligns with the HIPPO—Highest-Paid Person's Opinion. In the long run, you would likely stifle innovation and out-of-the-box thinking.

A more effective way to share

A manager as coach can and should share opinions when warranted. The key is to share them at the right time. Here are some sample sentence structures you can use to increase a sense of empowerment among team members and weave in your thinking without restricting others' creativity.

- I heard about this new initiative the other day from the other department. How does this affect our decision-making process?
- We have tried this method before and the results, I remember, were not so good. What has changed this time to make it a possible choice for us?
- We know from past experience the customers would push back on this type of decision. How can we approach it differently this time?
- This method has served us well over the years and I'm concerned that making a change now would require too much time and resources. What do you think?
- I think all these solutions you have proposed are great. Another factor I'd consider is people's readiness to embrace a new system. What are your thoughts?

Notice how these questions are worded. They all begin with a new piece of information that might have been missed and then quickly turn into open-ended questions that expand perspectives and stimulate thinking. The key is connecting the two parts together. This way, the manager would not just be dishing out advice.

> 'In a nutshell, advice is overrated. I can tell you something, and it's got a limited chance of making its way into your brain's hippocampus, the region that encodes memory. If I can ask you a question and you generate the answer yourself, the odds increase substantially.'
>
> Michael Bungay Stanier, *The Coaching Habit: Say Less, Ask More & Change the Way You Lead Forever*

In my ongoing work with Alya, we continuously look for opportunities to improve the quality of the questions she asks. One immediately noticeable change at first was that her listening and paraphrasing skills increased tremendously as she constantly applied these three things:

1. Assessing what her team understands
2. Determining what is not making sense
3. Then thinking of different ways to bridge the gap either by powerful questions or presenting the information before an open-ended question.

Self-Evaluation

- Recall the time when you had been creative and resourceful at work. What were the types of questions you were asked?
- How do you generally feel when someone gives you advice? Happy or annoyed? What makes the difference?
- What's going in your mind as you ask a question? Are you subconsciously expecting a 'correct' answer?
- Which category do your questions usually fall under? Open or closed?
- What do you notice about the quality of the responses you receive from others?
- How can you begin to ask better questions?

Your Reflections

Recall the time when you had been creative and resourceful at work. What were the types of questions you were asked?

How do you generally feel when someone gives you advice? Happy or annoyed? What makes the difference?

What's going in your mind as you ask a question? Are you subconsciously expecting a 'correct' answer?

Which category do your questions usually fall under? Open or closed?

What do you notice about the quality of the responses you receive from others?

How can you begin to ask better questions?

16.5. Career Conversations for Engagement

For those of you who are now people managers, how many of you were properly equipped to conduct productive career conversations? How many of you had fruitful and insightful career conversations? For the first five years of my career, the sum of all my career conversations came up to a total of thirty minutes. I am not kidding.

As a newbie at the workplace, I thought that was the norm for career conversations—we fill up the form, send it to each other, and then we meet at the office to sign it.

'Any questions?'

'No. Thanks.' I would quickly shuffle away to escape the awkwardness. I could sense that my reporting officer couldn't wait to get rid of me and get back to her work, either.

The understanding among leaders about this frequent topic of discussion—what makes a good career conversation—differs quite a lot. Most people conduct career conversations the way their managers did. For my first manager, I believe it was the script of a misguided Developer at play again and she was limited by what she knew. Career conversations and management process might also be influenced at company level. Every company has its own style and the quality varies massively, depending on the person driving the process.

You might think it's merely a conversation, but it could well be one of the most important conversations for employees. Given that career growth continues to be a key driving factor in employee engagement, leaders need to pay attention and gain the skills needed to conduct productive career conversations.

'Career Conversations are exactly what they sound like—discussions about someone's career with an emphasis on their long-term career aspirations. When done well, these should connect a person's past—gaining a detailed understanding of who they are and what motivates them at work through their life story—with their future; the wildest dreams they have for themselves at the pinnacle of their career.'

Russ Laraway, Vice President of People
Operations at Qualtrics

In such conversations, employees would be interested to learn the following:

- What did they do well?
- What are their opportunities for growth?
- What strengths do you see in them?
- How can they elevate themselves and increase their potential?

Managers can use career conversations to achieve three objectives:

1. Develop career plan
2. Assess employee motivations
3. Build trust and connection

Let us look at each of these in further detail.

Develop Career Plan

Career conversations can open up possibilities for employees and provide clarity on their future career paths. This is also the time for leaders to recognize good work, offer valuable feedback on areas of improvement, discuss potential job opportunities, or even plan out a training roadmap to bridge skill gaps.

In the 2021 People Management Report by Predictive Index, 17 per cent of employees said 'Provides Feedback' is one of the top five skills managers lack. Discussions on career progression paths are also an important milestone-check so that employees can make informed decisions about their future path, instead of leaving it to chance.

In the Leaders People Love Global Survey, 'recognizes me for good work' was rated the top behaviour from manager that increases employee happiness, with 52.3 per cent of respondents selecting this.

Assess Employee Motivations

Career conversations give employers an opportunity to get a more holistic view of their workforce, as well as identify potential for succession plans. This may involve understanding the motivation behind an employee's interests or exploring these interests further within the organization. All this information can then be used by leaders to create tailored development plans that fit each individual's needs and objectives. This is also a good time to gain deeper insights into each person's professional goals and aspirations. For instance, with the insights about employees' motivations, you could incorporate job rotations strategically so that you can retain your talent for longer by offering them valuable learning opportunities.

Leaders can also leverage this opportunity to help employees align and find purpose in their work, which is also the top priority for leaders (47 per cent), according to the 2022 State of Talent Optimization Report by Predictive Index.

Build Trust and Connection

'People don't care how much you know until they know how much you care.'

Dr John C. Maxwell

When managers show an interest in the holistic development of employees, employees tend to be more engaged as they see that their manager truly cares about them. Creating meaningful relationships based on trust helps employees grow, as they receive able guidance.

This results in a stronger connection within a team, while providing support to one another in achieving mutually beneficial outcomes.

Useful Questions for Career Conversations

Here is a list of useful questions you can use in career conversations:

- What did you like about the last project?
- What did you enjoy most?
- What do you think about the results?
- What was the biggest challenge in this project and how did you overcome it?
- If you had a chance to do it all over again, what changes would you make?
- What was the most important thing you have learned from the project?
- What have you learned about yourself through this project?
- What else would you like to learn or experience next?
- How do you see your work fitting into the larger picture?
- What other support do you need?
- How can I support you better?
- Other than the project outcomes, what else matters to you?
- How does this learning fit into your overall career aspirations or map?

Career conversations are important milestones for employees, so make it a point to develop the skills you need to conduct them effectively.

Agile Leadership Pointers

Nurture people's skills and attitudes. Similar to how we nurture plants, small actions of tender loving care bear fruits over time.

Self-Evaluation

- What's your personal experience with career conversations?
- How does that shape how you conduct such conversations with your team (now or in the future)?
- What would you like to include in your career conversations?
- How well do you understand your team's aspirations and life goals?
- What can you do differently to understand the whole person working with you?

Your Reflections

What's your personal experience with career conversations?
How does that shape how you conduct such conversations with your team (now or in the future)?
What would you like to include in your career conversations?
How well do you understand your team's aspirations and life goals?
What can you do differently to understand the whole person working with you?

16.6. Giving Feedback

'Can I give you some feedback?'

How does this question make you feel? Scared? Defensive because an attack might be coming? Stressed? Cringy? If you feel an uncomfortable emotion like one of these, you're not alone.

Timely

Giving and receiving feedback can be intimidating. This is why many shy away from giving feedback when they ought to—in a timely manner, meaning as soon as an incident takes place or when a behaviour is first observed.

Feedback comes in two types—positive and negative. Depending on your prior experience and upbringing, you might be comfortable with one, both, or neither. Feedback is, however, essential for a person to course-correct before things get out of hand.

Imagine a space shuttle being launched into space with the wrong bearings. The longer we delay correcting its course, the further off-track it will be. Good feedback needs to be timely.

Positive feedback is equally important because encouragement reinforces desired behaviours.

> 'Encouragement is oxygen for the soul. It takes very little effort to give it, but the return in others is huge.'
>
> Dr John C. Maxwell

Specific, Constructive, and Non-judgemental

Effective feedback is often specific and constructive. It's neutral, free of labels and assumptions or inference, and non-judgemental.

For instance, a feedback like 'I really appreciate your thorough thinking as you pointed out issues many of us missed' is better than 'Thanks for your thoughts'.

Likewise, a feedback like 'I noticed the updates are not always as prompt as we had agreed. This might affect how others perceive you. Can we talk about it?' is better than 'It looks like you are struggling with your work because your updates are late. Do you need help?' ('Struggling' is an assumption.)

To give specific and constructive feedback, a manager needs to be observant. Noticing how and what your team does is an important ability to develop. As a manager, when you can name specifics, your team will know that their hard work will not go unnoticed.

The following are some observations about the common techniques recommended for giving feedback.

Hamburger technique

In the 1980s, Mary Kay Ash, founder of Mary Kay Cosmetics, created what is now known as the 'hamburger' technique or 'feedback sandwich', where criticisms are layered between praises before and after, therefore sandwiched.

You may have heard of it, or even tried it. I do not use this technique as it is, but a version of it. Some experts have strongly condemned this technique and recommend using other approaches. Similarly, a few leaders I know have sworn against the 'feedback sandwich' and prefer to use a direct approach. Each approach has its merits. A direct approach is useful for instances where you have very few positive things to say. Instead of making something up to layer the criticisms, just speak directly to the issue. Fundamentally, use the method most attuned to your personality and audience. Remember the anatomy of building trustworthiness in your brand comprises authenticity, empathy and logic (see 'Theme X: Inspiring Trust'). If you are going to pepper your feedback with false praise first, it will erode your brand and trustworthiness.

If you use this sandwich technique or a variation of it, you can make it more effective by changing the sentence structure. I have observed people being motivated as a result of a feedback like that. Let me show you two examples and we can compare the difference.

Sandwich Technique—Example 1

'What you did on the presentation was great, <u>but</u> the analysis seems to have fallen short. Overall, it's a good presentation, so well done.'

The issue with feedback like this is the word 'but', which changes the meaning of the sentence. A few things can happen as a result of that. People may not believe the 'good' part because they might believe it to simply be a disguise for critical feedback. Anticipating an 'attack' raises walls of defence in their mind, which then might correspondingly lower their receptivity.

Another pitfall I have observed occurs when leaders themselves are uncomfortable with critical feedback, so they quickly rush through it. This undermines the severity of the negative but useful feedback if delivered calmly, slowly and factually.

Compare this now with example 2.

Sandwich Technique Modified—Example 2

'What you did on the presentation was great. I like how you presented the points with the audience in mind. What can make it even better is if the analysis were more holistic. It will paint an even more compelling case and become even more persuasive.'

In this case, I separated the praise from the 'criticism'; you can use 'and' instead of 'but' to reduce the sense of threat, and end with encouragement to inspire them to strive from good to great. Notice how I also stated a specific reason to support the praise, so it was just not simply 'air without substance'. What I want to convey is, 'based on what you have done today, you can be even better tomorrow'.

Agile Leadership Pointers

Good, constructive, and specific feedback is the fruit of superior observation skills.

State Criticism Directly When Due

In most cases, I begin my feedback sessions with something good. The caveat is that it must be true and not made-up—aligned with my belief about always being truthful, honest, and kind. In cases when there is nothing to praise, or if the issue is absolutely serious and demands the full attention of the listener, I will directly state my criticism.

It might sound something like: 'I noticed some serious issues with your recent piece of work. I need to let you know because it's important to all of us, you included. It looked like the guidelines were not followed and this needs to be rectified before we can share it with the client. Let's discuss it now.'

Notice I avoid words that would indicate blame as, ultimately, I want the listener to feel that I am being supportive of them without undermining the severity of the issue. When possible, I state a win-win intention. In this example, it's to help the listener achieve the best outcome.

Recall the earlier point about suspending judgement, so watch out for words that could sound judgemental. For instance, you'll want to avoid saying things like: 'Your recent piece of work was so bad' ('bad' is a judgement). 'Why can't you follow the guidelines?' (blame); 'Are you struggling?' (assumption).

Noticing Potential Talents Leads to Aspirational Development

In my opinion, one of the best things anyone can do for another fellow human being is to notice and recognize the potential in them. Having one's talents noticed does wonders for the human spirit. It makes one feel more determined to fully lean into a challenge and achieve the best possible result. It's as if the affirmation of a potential makes it seem achievable.

This is why one of my favourite words is the Sanskrit greeting 'Namaste'. There are many translations for it; the one I like most is, 'I see you and I honour you'. When you see someone for who they truly are, hope and self-efficacy rise.

In our society, it's far more common to receive criticism than sincere encouragement. The negativity bias runs deep in our DNA and our mind is naturally drawn towards something negative. In fact, most of us probably drew more attention as children when we got into trouble, than when we were cruising along. This is pervasively true in workplaces, too. When I speak to leaders about their strengths, they are often far more interested in focusing on their weaknesses. Even though affirming others might be a rare practice in certain cultures, I want to encourage you—a leader people love in formation—to spend more effort noticing potential talents in others. It will yield far greater benefits than criticism will.

> 'Praise is like sunlight to the warm human spirit; we cannot flower and grow without it. And yet, while most of us are only too ready to apply to others the cold wind of criticism, we are somehow reluctant to give our fellow the warm sunshine of praise.'
>
> Dale Carnegie, *How to Win Friends and Influence People*

I have used this technique many times and the results have been positive every time. I use it to encourage my children when they are learning something new. Overriding thoughts of fear and uncertainty, recognizing the potential in them and saying it out loud, helps them believe that success is possible. It gives them the motivation to try their hand at something hard albeit the discomfort, and raises their resilience to pick themselves up after each failed attempt, again and again. I apply this technique to the leaders with whom I work, for example, by highlighting what I see—how a leader might be deeply concerned about the well-being of his team members; how another might be thoughtful and diligent in making sound decisions. Naming the quality brings it to the top of the mind, reinforcing the best in that person.

When I was a teacher, I noticed that nothing lit up the eyes of my students more than the sentence, 'I believe in you'. *And all leaders were children once.*

All these are small acts leaders can easily incorporate into their methods to see higher engagement, commitment, and accountability in their team. This is an equally important technique for increasing innovation and lowering the fear of failure, as I will cover in the next section.

There is no greater desire in the world than to be *seen, heard, and understood*, so spend a little effort to notice talents around you and let people know of the light you see in them.

Agile Leadership Pointers

Ignite fires of resilience and drive in people by acknowledging the potential you see in them.

The Case of the Nasty and Unexpected Performance Rating

Have you ever met someone who was utterly angered and felt blindsided when they were given a poor performance rating?

Over the years, I have met many managers, commonly first-timers, who would lose sleep over an upcoming performance conversation. The reason? They would have given an unsuspecting fellow a low performance rating. In my opinion, the manager is usually responsible for matters reaching this state.

Career conversations—when done well—give people a helpful indication of how they are doing. Timely, constructive and actionable feedback tells them where they can improve. The lack of such conversations will set managers up for a most uncomfortable, confrontational appraisal, resulting in feelings of betrayal and anger.

No one should learn about their development gaps only at the end of the performance cycle. Similarly, no one should realize that he or she had been doing well all along only after they receive the once-in-a-year performance rating. If the true assessment of a person is not made known to them earlier, it's the manager who needs to take responsibility.

Agile Leadership Pointers

Keeping people informed about how they are being appraised and perceived helps them detect and act on gaps in a timely manner.

Key Points in a Snapshot

- A leader's job is to help people think and do better. Start by asking better questions that expand perspectives.
- Assigning tasks of the right difficulty and nature stretches people appropriately.
- Giving the answers away too quickly stunts growth and development.
- Getting angry when someone doesn't understand is not helpful. What they need is a building block to stack on top of their prior knowledge.
- Career conversations are meant to encourage career development. Don't skip it.
- Observe people carefully so you can give specific and actionable feedback.
- Keep people informed about how they're doing. No one should be surprised at receiving a bad performance rating.

Self-Evaluation

- Which type of feedback do you feel comfortable giving—positive or negative? How does that shape your leadership brand?
- How often do you give feedback?
- What is the impact of your feedback? Is it positive or negative?
- How do you personally feel about giving feedback? What does it mean?
- How do you prepare so that you can give useful feedback?
- How can you assess the effectiveness of your feedback?

Refer to https://leaderspeoplelove.com/resources
for more resources to increase your agility.

Your Reflections

Which type of feedback do you feel comfortable giving—positive or negative? How does that shape your leadership brand?
How often do you give feedback?
What is the impact of your feedback? Is it positive or negative?
How do you personally feel about giving feedback? What does it mean?
How do you prepare so that you can give useful feedback?
How can you assess the effectiveness of your feedback?

17

Theme V: Increasing Innovation by Lowering Fear of Failure

'Today's competitive landscape heavily relies on innovation. Business leaders must constantly look for new ways to innovate because you can't solve many problems with old solutions.'

Michael Boyles, Online Contributor, Harvard Business School

Research by McKinsey found in a poll of executives that 85 per cent of them agree that 'fear holds back innovation efforts often or always in their organization.' (Furstenthal et al 2022)

While fear is understandable, leaders need to understand that it's in direct competition with the spirit of innovation and risk-taking.

People typically experience different types of fear, all natural and part of the human experience. Some of the more common ones which even experienced and established leaders fall prey to, are fear of being ridiculed, fear of making mistakes, and fear of 'looking stupid'.

Some high-performing leaders even label themselves as 'anxious over-achievers' and have limited success in managing their reactions.

To understand how to overcome the mindsets that impede executives' dispositions towards innovation or anything that might seem risky, we need first to understand their fears. The aforementioned research by McKinsey named three types of fears that corporate executives experience more than others:

1. Fear of career impact and potential loss, where people tend to 'play it safe' rather than to innovate for fear of personal loss. This is typical of leaders who 'rely on tried-and-tested methods'—a criticism many leaders receive in their 360-assessment reports but struggle to do anything about.

2. Fear of uncertainty and loss of control, where leaders steer people towards safer projects where outcomes are perceived as more certain, or add to the pressure on their teams for assurances that the project will pay off. This creates pressure down the line, where people feel that they are expected to innovate but are not allowed to fail, which is demotivating and counter-productive.

3. Fear of criticism steers decision-makers towards tried-and-tested methods that are less likely to invite scrutiny or challenging questions. This gap in mindset at the level of top management causes dissent and friction within an organization.

> 'A new idea is delicate. It can be killed by a sneer or a yawn; it can be stabbed to death by a quip and worried to death by a frown on the right man's brow.'
>
> Ovid

However, continuously being paralysed by fear and treating past trends as predictors of future performance is a risky move. When assumptions are made with no regard for the changed or changing economic landscape, the cost of doing something that used to work but is no longer relevant, is high. This is why the first step of the Re4 Model, 'Reconstruct the Map', is crucial (See 2.4. Step Two: Outside-In Scan).

Leaders need first to recognize that change and innovation are not nice-to-haves but must-haves. Secondly, they need to accept that fear and uncertainty will be a perpetual part of leading in today's complex world.

True courage is not the absence of fear but proceeding in spite of it.

Many leaders need help in this area. In the following section, you will find some ways to increase innovation by reducing fear of failure and encourage considered assessment to minimize risk and potential loss.

Agile Leadership Pointers

There is no courage without fear, success without failure, or innovations without experiments.

17.1. How Executives Can Lower the Fear of Failure

Thomas Edison invented the light bulb successfully after failing 10,000 times. In his famous words, 'I have not failed. I've just found 10,000 ways that won't work.'

If Thomas Edison had succumbed to the fear of failure or risks, the world might well be shrouded in darkness still, or dependent on candlelight or kerosene lamps.

Anyone who has experienced successful innovation or is an advocate for innovation would know that failure—the ways it might not work out—is an essential part of the journey. We all know that innovation is important for organizational survival but when met with a high fear of failure, culminates in a confrontation where fear usually wins.

A bright spark of innovation snuffed out too early would only shroud the organization in darkness and slowly fade into irrelevance. Typically, the fastest way to kill innovation is to play the blame game.

Imagine a senior leader saying, 'Innovation is important and we encourage everyone to try new ways and take risks,' and then at the first sign of risk or imminent failure, quickly fall back into blaming, pointing fingers and demanding, 'Why did this happen? How could you let this mistake happen?'

It's unrealistic to promote innovation only when it's guaranteed to succeed. At the first sign of risk or failure, your first reaction matters (see 8.1.).

Here are some reframing that you could consider to lower your fear of failure and manage your reactions:

- Failures are simply ways that don't work.
- Where there is a risk of failure, there is also a possibility of success.
- Fear is a natural protective mechanism, so as long as you have prepared for the worst, you would have covered your bases.
- If you don't try, you'll never know if you'll succeed.

17.2. Increase Thoughtful Risk Management

Alya wanted to encourage her team to adopt a new system. Her team, however, much preferred tried-and-tested methods over the improvements she was trying to bring in.

Here are some of the worries expressed by her team:

- 'It is so complicated. What if I make a mistake?'
- 'The customers would find it too cumbersome to adopt this new system and get angry with us.'

She had been trying for months to get them to adopt the new system as it would elevate the quality of their work, shifting them away from manual, error-prone work to higher-value tasks that included more analysis and higher-order thinking. But the fear of making mistakes and reaping undesirable outcomes held them back.

When Alya raised this issue to me with a certain level of frustration, I gently reminded her that fear is a natural emotion. People instinctively resist change and try to maintain the status quo.

I encouraged her to turn these fears and worries into something useful, like thinking through the risks and taking action to address them. I offered some strategies she could try to encourage risk-taking in her team: reframing, challenging assumptions and mitigating risks.

1. **Reframing the definition of failure:** 'It's not wrong, only a different way of doing things.'
2. **Challenging assumptions or inferences that are groundless:** 'Let's try and find out together.'
3. **Counter fear of the unknown (what if's) with possibilities:** 'Introduce the potential joy of obtaining positive results.'
4. **Taking care of the possible downsides:** 'Take proactive measures to prepare for the worst-case scenario.'

Alya and I did a roleplay exercise to help her learn the technique of reframing. Alya played the role of her team members and I played the role of Alya.

Me: We've got the new system ready for your adoption. What's the progress?

Alya: Oh yes, we got that. We have not tried it yet because we are worried that the customers will find it cumbersome and get upset.

Me: I agree that it's important that the customers are satisfied (turning worry into a desire). Factually speaking, however, we haven't had them try the system yet, so we cannot know what they think for certain until they have tried it (turning worry into an action). What do you think?

Alya: We are afraid of the risks . . . What if we give them the wrong instructions? Why can't we just stick to the old one?

Me: I hear you. Giving customers the right set of access instructions is very important (turning worry into desire). I also understand the old one is more comfortable as we are more familiar with it. What if the new system, while still unfamiliar now, is even more beneficial for the customers and for us (introduce possibilities)?

Alya: I suppose there's a possibility . . .

Me: Yeah . . . I hear your considerations, though, I agree we need to help customers feel at ease with the system (reinforce desire).

How can we play the role of the guide (reframe their role) to help them more accurately so the migration is smoother?

Alya: I think we will have to try it together with them and walk beside them . . .

Me: I agree with you. It will be new, uncomfortable. There will be slip-ups, for sure, and all these are part of us familiarizing ourselves with the system so that we can help our customers adopt it too. To make sure we cover our bases, what are the possible scenarios that could happen, and how can we take care of them (thinking through actions and managing risks)?

Alya: I think as we try it out ourselves, the risks should be manageable as long as we start with the smaller accounts and do it step by step. Perhaps, we could also start with the customers who are more receptive and manage their expectations, to seek their understanding and patience.

Me: Great. Sounds like you got a plan worked out.

From the conversation above, you may observe the following:

When someone raises a concern, it's important to acknowledge and validate it instead of dismissing and negating them. Certain personalities are more conservative and cautious. Accept them as they are and build on your next step from their understanding. Depending on the individual's receptiveness, maturity, and personality, you can also offer a series of action steps.

These principles can also be applied when you influence upwards. First, understanding your stakeholders' risk profile and appetite, and then tailoring your approach to put them at ease, will increase your chances of nurturing innovation.

> 'As we are liberated from our own fear, our presence automatically liberates others.'
>
> Nelson Mandela

Key Points in a Snapshot

- Feeling fearful of the unknown is natural and so is the excitement of possibility.
- Executives, too, experience fear. With thoughtful risk management, we can increase the chances of proceeding with courage.
- Innovation and failed experiments always go hand-in-hand.

18

Theme VI: Facilitating Generative and Inclusive Conversations

Avoiding groupthink by asking open-ended questions and making better use of the coaching style helped Alya make real progress with her team. Their communication pattern became more dynamic. Where Alya once used to direct the conversation with a series of rapid-fire questions about the progress of work, their meetings have now become more participative.

In the past, whenever Alya introduced something new to her team, they would remain solemn and unresponsive. Once, on a virtual call, she paused her lengthy monologue to explain a decision and was met with total silence. Alya thought that perhaps she had lost her connection to the call, or that her mic had been on mute all the while and no one had heard her. Now, being able to convert the highly unproductive monologues into vibrant discussions was a refreshing and welcome improvement. It was like her leading with a coaching mindset and asking better questions injected life and enthusiasm into the people who would otherwise have laid dormant. Having more people chime in and add their perspectives improved the team's cohesion and understanding of how each person's work was connected to the bigger picture. It also increased Alya's confidence in facilitating high-quality team discussions. She's now ready to take discussions to the next level.

In the Leaders People Love Global Survey, 59.1 per cent of respondents selected 'facilitating inclusive and generative discussions' (third most-chosen option) as a competency they believe managers need to lead effectively in disruptive times.

On the following pages, I'll share some actionable ways you can use to develop this skill.

18.1. Use Specific Praise to Drive Behaviours

While the overall dynamics had improved, there was still a pattern that Alya noticed and was curious about. Whenever new interventions were brought to the table for discussion, the conclusion would almost always be aligned with what Alya initially had in mind.

'What is the point of our discussions if all the conclusions are exactly the same as what I had thought initially?' she asked. 'Or are we really so aligned that we all can agree on the same intervention? Is this a case of "great minds think alike"?' she quizzed. 'What if we are dangerously "group thinking" and missing out on other solutions we need to consider?'

I was very happy that Alya thought about these questions, as groupthink is indeed something leaders need to watch out for and mitigate its effects. While consensus is important, research has also shown that driving toward consensus-based solutions often kills innovation (Criscuolo et al 2016).

> 'Diversity drives innovation—when we limit who can contribute, we in turn limit the problems we can solve.'
>
> Telle Whitney, computer scientist,
> advocate and expert on 'women and technology'

Given that we naturally prefer people who are similar to us because they communicate in a way we can understand, we might also tend to show our approval and affirmation toward them more readily, compared to someone who seems different.

This is what Alya needed to pay attention to. As we dived deeper into how discussions unfolded, she was able to identify the exact moment when people converged on the same—her—solution.

She was doing a great job at contextualizing the issue and posing open questions to encourage divergent thinking. As people chimed in sporadically one after another, she would respond with a diplomatic smile and thank them for their input. But when someone said something that happened to be aligned with her sentiments, she would get very animated and enthusiastically share that she too, had the same thinking. The conversation thereafter would converge at that point and the discussion would abruptly come to close.

> '(Generic) Praise that contains little task-related information and is rarely converted into more engagement, commitment to learning goals, enhanced self-efficacy, or understanding about the task.'
>
> John Hattie and Helen Timperley, *The Power of Feedback*

Here was the issue: Alya had offered generic praise to someone who shared an idea that was different from hers and lavished specific praise on another who echoed her thoughts. Her behaviour in response to something new was lukewarm and highly energetic when someone spoke about something that aligned with what was on her mind.

As the leader of the group, she had also shared her HIPPO over-zealously. So while she set the stage for an open and healthy discussion, her over-enthusiasm at the 'right answer' shaped the team's responses. As a result, the unspoken message she had been subconsciously sending out was: *Your input is more valuable when it's aligned with mine.*

She had unknowingly encouraged people to guess the 'right' answer in her mind and quickly converge with it.

As we discussed this issue further, Alya realized that she had unknowingly steered the outcomes towards the very outcome she did not want—groupthink—leaving people guessing what the leader wanted and self-censoring if they anticipated rejection or disapproval.

Having learned and mastered the first part about inspiring innovation, what Alya could do next was to encourage more divergent thinking and not fall into past patterns. She could do better by doubling down on the following strategies:

- Encourage challenging the norms and status quo.
- Put the 'ideal' solution in the 'parking lot' first and evaluate other options.
- Clarify the 'why' of a solution before diving into the 'how'.
- Devise evaluation criteria agreed upon by the group based on the 'why.'

A few modifications I then offered to Alya were as below:

1. To avoid causing people to converge on her viewpoint too quickly, she must learn to moderate her excitement when someone seemed to 'get it right'. Instead, she needed to acknowledge that she shared the same thoughts (without showing too much excitement) and encourage a few more alternative views, before evaluating all the perspectives equally.
2. Be clear about the behaviours or qualities she wanted to encourage most and tailor her praises specifically. For example, to encourage new perspectives, the next time someone gave an innovative or out-of-the-box idea, she could say something like, 'Thanks for raising this new perspective. I have not thought of it before. Let's go a little deeper into that'; or 'Great thinking—this is something we have not tried before and I believe there's value in exploring it.'
3. Let her team take turns chairing the discussion and play the role of the leader, so that people would be less inclined to defer to her views.

Agile Leadership Pointers

To elevate perspectives, first expand them.

Self-Evalution

- Recall a time when your new idea was considered. How did you put it across?
- How do you usually respond to new thoughts and ideas?
- How often are new ideas heard and accepted in your organization?
- How can you ask questions that broaden people's perspectives?
- How do you know when opinions truly converge, or could your team members be feeling that raising alternative perspectives would be futile or unsafe? If so, how can you change that?
- What behaviours or qualities do you want to nurture in your organization or team?

Your Reflections

Recall a time when your new idea was considered. How did you put it across?
How do you usually respond to new thoughts and ideas?
How often are new ideas heard and accepted in your organization?
How can you ask questions that broaden people's perspectives?
How do you know when opinions truly converge, or could your team members be feeling that raising alternative perspectives would be futile or unsafe? If so, how can you change that?
What behaviours or qualities do you want to nurture in your organization or team?

18.2. Techniques that Elevate the Quality of Conversations

The danger with generative and inclusive conversations is that at times, they can drag on and the meeting could lose momentum. Leaders need to set up the right parameters so that conversations and discussions are productive, elevating, as well as time-efficient.

Better Work Institute surveyed 182 senior managers across industries in 2017 and discovered that:

- 65 per cent said meetings keep them from completing their own work.
- 71 per cent said meetings are unproductive and inefficient.
- 64 per cent said meetings come at the expense of deep thinking.
- 62 per cent said meetings are missed opportunities to bring the team closer together.

With such stark statistics and an 80 per cent chance that you are time-poor, according to Ashley Whillans's book, Time Smart (2020), four out of five adults wished they had more time to do what they needed to do. Having too little time is also associated with poor health, low productivity and bad relationships. Learning to facilitate generative and inclusive conversations efficiently is a skill that will deliver a good payoff.

The techniques shared here will help make your meetings productive and efficient. Energize your team and help them grow and develop in these instrumental workplace conversations. When the conversations at your organization are rewarding and enlightening, people will naturally come prepared, ready to participate and engage.

It's not how much time you spend on an activity but how you spend the time that determines your outcomes.

Dig Further and Unpack Definitions

Here is a typical conversation.

Manager: What do you think about this initiative?

Team: It's okay.

If you were the manager in this conversation, what would you do next?

1. Say, 'Good, let's proceed with this initiative.'
2. Ask further questions to discover the real answer behind 'it's okay'.

Many leaders lamented that some of their initiatives were derailed by misinterpretation or misunderstanding of what had been agreed on. Friction arises when projects are set in motion only to grind to a halt because not everyone understands what was agreed on or need to be done in the same way.

When kicking off innovative initiatives, it becomes even more important to ensure alignment and common understanding. You want to use this as an opportunity to highlight that doing something new together can be rewarding, so it becomes especially important to create more positive experiences than negative ones. This is how you can build people's appetite for change.

So in a conversation like this, construct a fuller understanding of the agreement by not taking people's responses at face value. Instead, dig deeper so you can hear the real message behind a generic response. For example:

Generic Response	Dig Deeper by Asking . . .
It's okay	What do you mean?
I understand	What have you understood?
I think it's good	Good in what way?
I'm afraid there will be resistance	From whom and in what form?
I'm not sure people will agree	Who are these people?

Generic Response	Dig Deeper by Asking . . .
They said they are aligned with our direction	What does it mean to have them align with us?
It's complicated	Tell me more.
They said they will do it as soon as they have the bandwidth	When is that and how much bandwidth are we talking about here?

As you ask these questions, you will find people thinking a little deeper, responding a little more thoughtfully, and becoming more accountable and committed. All these little steps you take are also laying the groundwork for seamless collaboration.

Use the Power of Silence

Many leaders I know are uncomfortable with silence. Especially the silence that ensues after they ask a question. They hurriedly fill the vacuum with one question after another, until finally, they give up and supply their own answers.

This is a trap and a behavioural pattern leaders need to be aware of and avoid. Repeat this behaviour pattern enough times and you will begin to see its negative consequences. Attendees in the meeting would know that if they were asked a difficult question, all they needed to do was to look thoughtful, wait for three seconds, and the boss would answer the question himself.

Here is another painfully ineffective yet frequent pattern of behaviour which might play out as follows:

'So with the data we now have, what shall we do?'

(*3 seconds of silence*)

'I mean, we gotta do something, right?'

(*More silence*)

'Does anybody have any idea what we shall do next?'

(*Dead silence*)

'For example, how about we do A or B?'

(*3 seconds later . . .*)

'Like, which one is better? A? Maybe A.'

(Another 3 seconds later . . .)

'Any questions?'

(Crickets . . .)

'No questions?'

(3 seconds later . . .)

'Okay, it's decided then. We will go with A. Next item on the agenda?'

When the leader asks a tirade of questions as in the scenario above, people generally feel confused about which question they are expected to answer. Or they may wonder if the leader really wanted to hear from them at all, since he answered his own questions.

Drawing insights from education, an article from Edutopia (McCarthy 2018) suggests teachers to wait for five to fifteen seconds, especially when the question they are asking is difficult or needs more processing.

This strategy is applicable in the workplace as well. In my experience, you might want to wait for at least ten seconds before interjecting.

If you are uncomfortable with silence, it will take a while for you to get used to waiting for answers. To deal with the silence and normalize it, you can try the following:

- Look thoughtful, smile encouragingly.
- Assume that people are thinking. If it helps, imagine the cogs in their heads turning.
- Ten seconds later, if there is still silence, you can ask if the question was clear (sometimes the listener may have been distracted for a second and missed the question).
- Watch out for people who look like they have something to say. They might just be waiting for you to call upon them. Sometimes all it takes is an eye contact and a raised brow.
- Watch out for people who are avoiding eye contact with you. They too, might be uncomfortable with your question. You could say something like, 'I notice you are avoiding making eye contact with me. (laugh) I really want to hear your thoughts. Tell us what's on your mind?'
- You could name some of their possible thoughts or objections out loud. That usually gets people to feel less reserved and

some might start nodding. Then that is your cue to invite people to share their thoughts.

Another strategy you might find helpful is W.A.I.T., an acronym for 'Why Am I Talking?' You might find this useful if you tend to want to fill the void of silence with your voice, just to reduce the awkwardness in the room. Before you start talking (and interrupting thinking time), you can ask yourself: Why Am I Talking? Does my talking here add value to the conversation or help the team, or is it counterproductive?

Self-Evaluation

- What vague answers do you habitually accept, but can probe for greater clarity?
- How comfortable are you with silence now?

Your Reflections

What vague answers do you habitually accept, but can probe for greater clarity?

How comfortable are you with silence now?

Hear the Quiet Voices

Quite a few leaders I work with are introverts. Contrary to common perception, the mind of an introvert is abuzz with a flurry of thoughts and activity—it's not a vacuum of silence. In many workplaces, introverts tend to be missed or glossed over, as they tend to remain silent instead of speaking up. For the organization's benefit, leaders should create opportunities for all voices to be heard, not only the loudest ones.

Employees who tend to be quieter might simply need a little more time to get comfortable or to feel safe. Not everyone can express their thoughts instantly, but once they do, you might find their opinions to be quite insightful. I have also learned over the years that everyone has something useful and insightful to share, and it's up to you, the leader, to make them feel safe enough to speak.

Here are some ways you can draw them out:

- Utilize small group discussions to get people to share and speak in a safe environment first.
- Explore different ways to collect viewpoints.
- Get people to summarise and share the viewpoints they hear from the others.
- Affirm and validate a viewpoint, then invite the person to go deeper.

In a large group, it's easy to bypass people who are quieter, so pay particular attention to this. You also want to do gatekeeping to rein in over-zealous people who talk all the time.

A productive conversation is one where many voices share the bandwidth and actively chime in, not one dominated by just a few.

> *Good conversations are diverse and inclusive.*

Apply the Power of Observation

At times, leaders know when something is not right, but don't know what to do about it. Many try to ask for feedback directly but when it feels unsafe or politically incorrect, a direct question only yields evasive answers.

> *Direct questions only work when you have*
> *sufficient trust and psychological safety.*

What can leaders do then when they sense that not everybody is on the same page? I suggest tapping into your power of observation. Use any or all of your five senses.

Name the elephant

Think of this method as related to naming the elephant in the room, because most of the time, everybody is painfully aware that there is an elephant but no one has the guts to call it out. As the leader, you are in the best position to do so. Calling out the elephant is a strong conversation starter and invites constructive debate that will help move the conversation forward.

Using your power of observation through your senses, this is what you might like to say:

- **Sight:** 'I can see some of you are uneasy about this. Would you like to share more? It will really help us move forward.'
- **Hearing:** 'I can hear you are upset. Let me know how you feel about this so we can help.'
- **Gut:** 'I sense some reservation in the room. Let's talk about it.'
- **Touch:** 'It seems like what I'm saying isn't landing/clicking for you. Tell me more and help me understand.'

Naming the elephant in the room can advance your conversations rapidly. It also takes courage and guts and I believe you have it in you, so go for it!

Collective build

A lot of leaders try the above techniques and begin to see results. The initial success makes them hungry for more. One of the things they begin to notice is that people talk to the leader instead of one another. This is what I call a hub-and-spoke model, where the leader is at the centre of the conversation and everyone takes turns speaking to the leader in a collective setting.

There is nothing wrong with a hub-and-spoke model, as it's often the starting point for getting people to speak up comfortably. Hub-and-spoke is definitely better than monologues and announcements disguised as meetings.

As you hone your ability to facilitate discussions, imagine passing a ball around the room. Each time someone speaks, he is holding the metaphorical ball. The ideal case you want to create is for the ball to be passed from person to person, without you touching it in order to pass it on.

Agile Leadership Pointers

The quality of your team conversations determines your team's results.

One of the ways to create a collective build is to pass the conversation on to the next person. Here are some ways you can do it. Whenever someone raises an interesting point, try any of the following:

- 'Who else agrees with this? Let's go deeper into that.'
- 'I hear you. What else?' (Look at others.)
- 'Who has a different viewpoint? Help us understand how you see it.'
- 'Uhmm hmm . . .' and direct your gaze elsewhere. The ball needs to go elsewhere without you touching it.
- Smile and nod, then sit back to indicate that someone else has the ball now.

Self-Evaluation

- At your meetings, which one describes you better: Conversation Igniter or Facilitator?
- Imagine the conversation as an energy flow. What happens to the energy when you are present and absent?
- How can you make the energy flow on its own without the need for you to keep it going?

Your Reflections

At your meetings, which one describes you better: Conversation Igniter or Facilitator?
Imagine the conversation as an energy flow. What happens to the energy when you are present and absent?
How can you make the energy flow on its own without the need for you to keep it going?

18.3. Useful Coaching and Facilitation Questions

If leading with the coaching style is new to you, you might feel overwhelmed. Many of my clients ask for a list of sample questions they can ask, and so I have compiled them for you here.

Questions to Encourage Constructive Debates

Agreeing to disagree is not a healthy resolution. We can use it to prevent arguments with someone but in a highly collaborative environment, agreeing to disagree, to me, only reinforces divides which cannot be bridged. To be inclusive of diverse views, you can attempt to get people to establish common ground where both viewpoints would be valid.

Questions you can try:

- 'Noted that we have different points of view. What can we agree on?'
- 'There's value in both viewpoints. What conditions will make both equally valuable?'
- 'I can see both of you have the same goal. What if we were to walk in each other's shoes? How might your perspectives change?'
- 'How might conditions change so we can reach a consensus or compromise?'
- 'How might taking either route aid or hinder our progress towards the common goal?'

Questions that Encourage Thinking and Clarity

Sometimes, I meet people who are not immediately able to dissect and present an issue clearly. This depends on their mental models. Since thinking aloud is valuable to many people, the leader can play the role of a thinking partner and ask questions to help the person gain clarity. These may be:

- 'What is the real problem?'
- 'How are you feeling about this?'
- 'What makes this an issue?'

- 'What do you need at this moment?'
- 'Who else do we need to involve?'
- 'What other perspectives or reasons might there be?'
- 'What else do we need to know?'
- 'How do we know what we know is true and valid?'
- 'What have we not considered and need to do so?'
- 'What is the biggest challenge that needs to be solved to move forward?'

Questions that Improve the Quality of Solutions

- 'What might be some of the unintended consequences of implementing this solution?'
- 'Who else's perspectives do we need to consider before implementing this?'
- 'What are some existing solutions we can tap on before creating brand new solutions?'
- 'How will we know if this solution will work?'
- 'What evidence will we need to look for to validate this solution?'
- 'What will people say if this solution were to work?'
- 'How else can we mitigate this problem?'
- 'What is the cost versus benefit of this solution?'
- 'When will this solution cease to be right for us?' (aka 'when do we pull the plug?')
- 'What groups of people may be disproportionately affected by this solution and why?'
- 'Who else do we need to hear from, in order to resolve this issue or achieve the goal?'

Questions that Assess Current Understanding

- 'What do you observe?'
- 'What patterns are you seeing?'
- 'How are the parts connected?'
- 'What else influences the reality?'
- 'What potential obstacles are there?'

- 'What else will make decision-making difficult?'
- 'What have we tried in the past that might be useful in this instance?'

Questions to Uncover Motivations and Aspirations

- 'What was your happiest moment at work and why?'
- 'Which project were you proudest of and why?'
- 'What do you value most at work? Name three.'
- 'What is the next skill you wish to develop?'
- 'What do you wish you had more of at work?'
- 'What do you wish you had less of at work?'
- 'What does the next level in your career look like?'
- 'What is one thing that will radically change your effectiveness and satisfaction at work?'

For more great questions and a guide on how to ask better questions, refer to Michael Bungay Stanier's book, *The Coaching Habit: Say Less, Ask More and Change the Way You Lead Forever* (2016).

Key Points in a Snapshot

- As a leader, your behaviour drives group habits. Moderate your excitement and disapproval accordingly.
- Consciously increase diversity of views before converging onto a decision.
- Dig deeper and go beyond superficial responses.
- Silence is thinking time for your team.
- Leverage the power of observation to advance difficult conversations.

19

Alya's Outcome

In my work with Alya, we focused on the Developer and its themes. In her team, she had to deal with issues of low appetite for change and a learning curve that was too flat and slow for Alya's need for speed. She needed to rapidly upskill and elevate her team's competency as she prepared for a role expansion that would thin her attention on them further.

Painfully aware that she could only accomplish so much by herself, she realized she needed to change her approach. Instead of sticking to the only methods she knew—telling and repeating herself—she began to apply the core principle of the Developer:

Lead others the way they want to be led. Teach people the way they need to be taught. Engage them the way they want to be engaged.

Alya spent time observing and getting to know her team better and began to figure out what made them tick and how to motivate them to learn. She began to engage with them more effectively.

It was difficult at first. She armed herself with questions and adopted a coaching mindset to expand thinking and deepen thought, but some questions bounced right off their closed minds. She was frustrated at the seeming lack of improvement, but she exercised much-needed patience. This was like working with hardened soil too parched and cracked after years of neglect for water to seep in. With consistency, Alya took small steps to prepare her team to become more receptive, watering the ground now and again—encouraging new behaviours and thinking patterns, while always listening to their concerns. She was the firm but patient hand guiding her team to think better and broader, so that they may begin to evolve and change their ways of working.

With the power of intention, Alya fully leveraged every touch point to stretch their thinking. Over time, little by little, the hard soil began to soften.

One of Alya's proudest moments was when a team member began chairing meetings and using open-ended questions to encourage thinking out of the box. They formulated better solutions than before and were comfortable trying new ways. As more people began driving positive changes and challenging one another's thinking, the team also adopted the new system she had been trying to set in place for months. They were even able to anticipate issues and alert Alya to them.

Nine months later, for the first time ever, Alya went on a silent retreat without her devices or work. Twelve days later, her team was still running the show collaboratively. She finally felt ready to take up the new role.

THE STRATEGIST

SUSTAINING EXCELLENCE WITH JOY

I kept hamsters as pets when I was young. As a child, I would always watch them sleep, drink, eat, and of course, run on the wheel. It was my favourite pastime after a long day.

I was fascinated by the relationship between the hamster and its wheel. Every hamster I had seemed to be obsessed with its wheel. Once it got on the wheel, the hamster would run as fast as its little legs would allow.

The faster the hamster ran, the quicker the wheel spun. It was like the hamster was trying to break the wheel and in turn, the wheel was trying to outrun the hamster.

Every day, the hamster would run as fast as it could, spinning the wheel faster and faster. The moment the wheel hit terminal velocity, the entire hamster cage would shake vigorously, rattling the wobbly shelf I had at that time, creating a ruckus in the house.

That would be the moment I had been waiting for. The 'victor' every time was the wheel, for we all know the hamster could never break the wheel. It was always the one that got thrown off because it got too slow to keep up with the wheel.

Almost compulsively and predictably, the little furball would repeat the exact routine. Undeterred, it would once again climb into the wheel and begin this unproductive cycle of spinning the wheel until it gets thrown off, accomplishing absolutely nothing except exhaustion.

As you reflect on this, do you also see yourself as a hamster on a wheel in some parts of your life?

20

Why the Strategist Is a Leader People Love

Getting more done with less is a big idea that motivates the Strategist. This voice focuses on high-yielding activities that will drive results for the organization. Instead of being confused and distracted by myriad ideas, the Strategist cuts through the noise and helps others prioritize, making work manageable and sustainable while achieving great outcomes seemingly effortlessly.

The Strategist also leverages resources carefully, be it people, talent, time, connections or opportunities. The Strategist dreams big and is motivated by hairy, audacious goals. But the Strategist is also connected to reality. Knowing that working harder and harder is not the way as it's not sustainable, the Strategist always seeks a better way.

The top agenda for the Strategist is to change the way workplaces operate. With a new mindset, the Strategist endeavours to design better strategies and ensure that achieving better results while operating with diminishing resources is not a dream but a reality.

Such is the effect of a Strategist.

Refer to https://leaderspeoplelove.com/resources for more resources.

21

Meet Joo Hwee

A Senior Leader in Technology Who Believes in a Better Way to Work and Live

'Every minute of my time is filled with something—so many high-stake decisions to make, so much guidance to give. It feels like I'm the brain and the rest of the organization is the arms and legs. It's simply not sustainable,' Joo Hwee lamented as we began the session with an energy check.

If this sounds like you, you might find many commonalities between Joo Hwee and yourself.

Joo Hwee was a senior leader in technology, at the forefront of innovation. Due to his depth of knowledge and clear understanding of the bigger picture, he was a highly valued member of the organization, where everybody wanted his input on anything and everything strategic—which comprised nearly everything—since he was in the most futuristic and cutting-edge arm of the business.

He used to enjoy the sense of importance as he believed in the work, and was happy to be able to make a difference. But of late, he began to feel increasingly constrained and trapped by his professional circumstances.

Interesting developments were happening in his field and he felt the strong tug of curiosity to venture into them, to sharpen his knowledge and skills, and rub shoulders with the 'giants' or the visionary innovators, but . . . he simply had no time or energy left after his work day. Nearly all his waking hours were spent on work— giving advice, dishing out directives and instructions. Having a patient and understanding spouse was a boon. She had, at first, tolerated his demanding job, then accepted it and finally resigned herself to fate. He was an absent parent and partner—they both knew it.

Joo Hwee had long since given up hopes about changing his unsustainable work schedule. However, something changed after the global pandemic. Call it post-traumatic event growth, if you will, but he began to wonder if there was a way to get out of the relentless and punishing hamster wheel and stop the insane spinning. He began to question if high performance can truly be joyous and sustainable if it inevitably resulted in long hours and total fatigue.

Joo Hwee's growing sense of dissatisfaction needed to be addressed. We also had to work out a new strategy for him so that he would continue to contribute fully to the organization. Joo Hwee is a knowledgeable and valuable resource, and to lose a leader like him for any reason would be a deep loss, and we needed to prevent that.

22

Theme VII: Fostering Strategic Thinking for a Culture of Sustainable Excellence

The importance of developing strategic thinking in organizations cannot be overstated. It involves the ability to think and plan for the long-term goals of an organization, rather than focusing on short-term, immediate goals. It enables organizations to anticipate the future and make decisions based on the best available information. Strategic thinking emphasizes the ability to understand the big picture and assess potential outcomes, rather than react to changes.

When unexpected situations erupt and multiple priorities clamour for the leaders' attention, holding the mental space for strategic and forward thinking becomes even more crucial. Leaders need to constantly guard against these two threats: being reactive and not noticing when plans have become outdated.

Strategic thinking is essential for any organization that wants to remain competitive and successful in the ever-changing business environment. It's indispensable for leaders who want to maximize the correlation between effort and impact.

The Strategist is constantly curious about the relationship between results, and time and effort. By picking the best activities to engage in, the Strategist directs investment into areas that result in the maximum and meaningful impact, bringing about happiness in the workplace.

22.1. If Time Were a Field

I heard this story from someone, years ago during a webinar. The topic of the webinar was prioritization and the speaker had used this metaphor to illustrate his point: 'If time were a field, what would your field be filled with? Weeds? Or flowers?'

I love this question, for it invoked a strong visual image—a field full of weeds strikes fear in leaders' hearts. It also illustrates the importance of tending your field (or garden, if you like) because weeds, like silent viruses or sickness, can insidiously invade your territory. By the time you realize it, a substantial segment of your precious field will have been overrun by invasive weeds.

Unlike how many people would approach the topic, I always look at prioritisation not as a function of time but as a function of energy and attention. Investing your energy and attention in the right matters is the strategic approach.

For busy, overwhelmed Joo Hwee, even more so. He thought about his team as well—they came into meetings poorly prepared as they too were hopping from one meeting to the next. As a result, despite the many minutes they spent together, they often had frustratingly little to show. As Joo Hwee thought about his field, probably imagining what other undesirable organisms were inhabiting it, he came to a conclusion.

He had been too careless about who, where and what he spent his time on. Such behaviour did not help his team either. He had wanted to help them carve time out for more meaningful endeavours, as the precious minutes and hours squandered away in unproductive meetings sapped their energy more than offered them rewards. At Joo Hwee's level of responsibility, time, energy, and attention were luxuries. He needed to conserve his resources. Should he have spent his time and foresight on other, more suitable areas, he could have created the greatest impact to benefit the wider community.

A gear spinning rapidly, freewheeling, is busy, but its activity is not productive. Unless the gear is connected to other gears and used to turn something else that did meaningful work, its busyness leads to nothing.

Busyness is not importance.
Activity is not productivity.
Effort is not contribution.

Self-Evaluation

- If time were a field, what is in yours? Weeds or flowers?
- Being helpful and taken for granted, which type applies to you now?
- How will you recalibrate where you spend your time, energy, and attention so that every minute is well-spent?

Your Reflections

If time were a field, what is in yours? Weeds or flowers?
Being helpful and taken for granted, which type applies to you now?
How will you recalibrate where you spend your time, energy, and attention so that every minute is well-spent?

22.2. Beware of the Weeds

Many leaders rise through the ranks due to subject-matter mastery. By quickly learning the ropes and demonstrating unparalleled knowledge in a certain domain, they formulate a way to be successful by being among the most knowledgeable persons in the room. Usually, these leaders are also strong in operational strategies, have ample ability to be meticulous, resilient and thorough, and to work as a team.

Such excellent and consistent performance would help them be entrusted with greater responsibilities and learning and stretching opportunities (recall *The Peter Principle* reference from Chapter 1). All is usually fine until the scope is enlarged so much that the old way of operating simply ceases to be effective. As ineffectiveness creeps in, slowly, it can initially be mitigated by working harder, faster, or longer. But the day does come when the leader realizes that harder, faster, or longer no longer works.

This is not unlike the fable about the frog who sits in a pot of slowly boiling water, unaware that conditions are becoming less and less favourable until it's far too late. The day comes, gradually but surely, when meticulousness and efficiency stop being blessings and instead turn into curses. The leader is stuck doing more and delving deep into everything. They get caught in the busyness trap.

To get out of the trap and reverse their waning effectiveness, something else needs to happen. Joo Hwee was no exception.

Navigating Joo Hwee's Conundrum

One of the feedback Joo Hwee received in his 360 report was 'being too detail-oriented' and that he should focus on other areas, like fostering relationships with external partners. At first, he was annoyed.

'Calling me too detail-oriented! Who was the one who got all those projects going? How could I have done them if not for my being meticulous! Now they are asking me to tone it down.'

'What got you here, won't get you there.'

Marshall Goldsmith, one of the
world's top gurus in leadership

As I believe working harder, faster, and longer are not sustainable models of working, I had to challenge Joo Hwee. 'There's the question about balancing breadth, depth, quality, and accuracy. How can you increase quality and accuracy yet maintain breadth and depth?'

'I don't know. What I have always done is to ask all the questions, poke holes in their plans and see if it's, indeed, a watertight plan. That's precisely the issue, isn't it—people feel like it's too time-consuming to work out the plans.'

A reframe I offered to Joo Hwee was as follows:

- To get high quality and accuracy, you can comb through all the weeds together, or you can just you can get more eyeballs on the weeds.
- To manage a wide breadth, you can cover all the parts, or simply focus on the big ideas of each part.

Some questions I encourage leaders in this situation to think about are:

- What questions do you need to ask so that you know enough about what is going on and not get lost in the details?
- As you ask the questions, are those for your benefit or your teams' benefit? (Are you satisfying your curiosity, or does everyone really need to know all those details?)
- What are the must-know, want-to-know, and do-not-need-to-know information?

22.3. What's Your Highest-Yielding Activity?

'Joo Hwee, given your seniority and the significance of your insights to the organization, what is the greatest value you bring?' During one of our conversations, I asked Joo Hwee as he breathlessly recounted all the meetings he had sat through, filling up his calendar—and mind—with tons of information but not necessarily feeling stimulated or inspired.

'Hmmm . . . my mission is to help the people succeed . . .'

'Yes, yes, I got that. But if we are talking about picking products to invest in now, where can you create the highest yield possible, based on what you are capable of doing? There are many ways to apply yourself, right? So what is that single highest-yielding activity you *need* to do?'

This is a question all leaders need to answer.

All of us operate within the same parameters—we all have twenty-four-hour days. Everyone is equal in this aspect, and if we want to raise our performance and maximize our results, we need to re-examine and validate these fundamental relationships:

- More time = more results;
- Working harder and faster = better performance;
- Activity = productivity.

These three relationships are generally true, although perhaps only at the earlier stage of our lives and careers.

Agile Leadership Pointers

Maximizing your results by having everyone spend most of their time on their highest-yielding activity.

Across the span of a person's career, the highest-yielding activity changes.

For example, the highest-yielding activity for an individual contributor might be to learn the ropes of the job, do it well and deliver results. For a manager leading a team, it might be to create an environment where people can do their jobs well and deliver, while developing the skills and attitudes that would ensure their success. For a senior leader, depending on the scope of their influence, the highest-yielding activity would differ.

Recognizing how we can add value is one way to elevate our mindset. In doing so, we attract new possibilities and outcomes.

> 'A man's mind may be likened to a garden, which may be intelligently cultivated or allowed to run wild; but whether cultivated or neglected, it must, and will, bring forth. If no useful seeds are put into it, then an abundance of useless weed seeds will fall therein, and will continue to produce their kind.'
>
> James Allen, *As a Man Thinketh*

Asking Joo Hwee this question helped him recognize that he needed to apportion his time and energy more strategically so that he could engage in his highest-yield activities. With the changes, his ecosystem began shifting towards another level of optimal performance.

Self-Evaluation

- What is your highest-yielding activity? (Think about your innate talents)
- How much of your energy and attention do you invest on your highest-yielding activity daily?

Your Reflections

What is your highest-yielding activity? (Think about your innate talents)
How much of your energy and attention do you invest on your highest-yielding activity daily?

22.4. Remove the Invisible Lid

I once heard a tale about training fleas to perform in a circus (a popular entertainment said to exist between 1500s–1800s). At first, I thought, 'What a tall tale! How could one train a flea? Or could they?'

After checking with a few sources, I found a video on YouTube. Here's how it was said to have been done. For context: The fleas were larger than the ones found on pets so the art died out as hygiene standards improved.

How to Train a Flea

First, place the fleas in a large glass jar. Next, cover the jar with the lid. Leave the fleas undisturbed. After three days, you can safely remove the lid and voilà! Now you have a bottle of trained fleas.

You can remove the lid, or even the bottle. The trained fleas will continue to leap as though the invisible lid were still present. That's not all! Any offspring produced by the trained fleas would also adhere to the same self-imposed boundary.

Isn't it amazing that in just three days, the fleas would permanently lose their natural ability to jump forty to hundred times higher than their body length and would forever be limited by the confines of the jar?

So here's the question for you: Who is more difficult to train? Humans? Or fleas?

'A man is literally what he thinks, his character being the complete sum of all his thoughts.'

James Allen, *As a Man Thinketh*

Navigating Joo Hwee's Conundrum

One of the first things Joo Hwee needed to do was to create greater bandwidth, but it was challenging as he was overwhelmed by the sheer number of problems he was given to solve: 'Why are there so many problems that require my attention?' I often have to remind leaders that if everything is burning, you need to look for the root cause.

Joo Hwee, as insightful, knowledgeable, and sharp as he was, was well-loved by his team, for all they had to do was to offer him any 'unsolvable' problem and he would be able to find a solution in a heartbeat. Joo Hwee had become an expert at solving others' difficult problems and was always happy to help, but he was badly overburdened. As we unpacked the issue, Joo Hwee began to understand what he felt most disturbed by.

First, he had some of the brightest minds on his team and yet, he was often the one left to offer solutions. It seemed like these high-potentials had lost their edge or acumen, and become too reliant on Joo Hwee. He could see that this was untenable for the organization.

Joo Hwee felt the weight of decision-making that had fallen on his shoulders. He was well aware that he was not infallible; one wrong judgement call could lead to dire consequences.

Second, being undeniably good at solving problems had been a frictionless way of working, but it was not good for his teammates' development. His eagerness and efficiency in solving difficult issues had impeded their potential and growth. From their perspective, Joo Hwee made their work smoother, faster and better. All they had to do was to surface the issues and pass them over to Joo Hwee to work his magic. It was a pattern that worked.

I shared with Joo Hwee the story about how fleas were said to be trained, and asked for his thoughts. He could understand his team's perspectives. He had made himself so accessible and they were only too happy to come into his office to seek guidance—excellent for his engagement and approachability, but bad for the team's growth and organization's future.

But continuing this way of working was also detrimental for Joo Hwee, as it clogged up his bandwidth, both in time and mindspace, preventing him from focusing on important strategic matters, which was to the detriment of the organization.

Taking over the responsibility of problem-solving too much also places a lid over the high-potentials—instead of stretching themselves, they get stuck maintaining things at their current levels (Joo Hwee's level). Over time, they could lose the ability to learn and increase their potential. The ultimate danger is that when the time comes for the high-potentials to step up and take the reins, they would have lost the advantage of time and exposure to enhance their fine business acumen and the wisdom needed to lead the organization competently.

The immediate takeaway for Joo Hwee was for him is to stop being the lid. That meant he needed to step back so that the high-potentials could step up, jump higher than they used to, or as high as they could. I also suggested that Joo Hwee dial down on how promptly he offered a solution and let his team experience some healthy struggle.

This would put his team in a learning zone between the comfort and fear zones (referring to Vygotsky's 'Zone of Proximal Development', where people learn to do something unfamiliar with assistance, eventually developing the permanent ability.)

> *Q: What is the most precious part of learning?*
> *A: The joy of learning something for the first time.*

Joo Hwee was a little uncomfortable about the suggestion but a chain of events conspired to force his hand. He was tasked to lead a delegate overseas and as he arrived, his laptop promptly crashed, leaving him unable to respond to his emails.

Five days after his team had first hollered for help, they responded with a follow-up email that said:

'Hey, Joo Hwee, no worries about the issue. We managed to sit down with the other party and resolve it. Enjoy your trip. Please take care. See you next week!'

His learning and takeaway? Sometimes the best way to help people learn how to solve their problems is to step back.

> *Be available to render help when constructive;*
> *be mindful not to rescue when it isn't.*

Simply by stepping back strategically, problems were resolved without taking up Joo Hwee's time and mindspace. His team put their heads together, helped one another and gained valuable battle experience in becoming good, wise leaders in the future.

Self-Evaluation

- In your eagerness and kindness to help others, have you also unknowingly robbed them of the chance to explore, discover, and grow?
- If you have a tendency to rescue others, consider for whose benefit that behavior is – yours or theirs?
- As high-performing leaders, how can you help your followers be more high-performing than you in the future?

Your Reflections

In your eagerness and kindness to help others, have you also unknowingly robbed them of the chance to explore, discover, and grow?

If you have a tendency to rescue others, consider for whose benefit that behavior is – yours or theirs?

As high-performing leaders, how can you help your followers be more high-performing than you in the future?

22.5. If You Had Only One Match

Many leaders I know are excited about the future. All the possibilities about what could be and the abundant potential out there in the universe waiting to be realized—the true joy of turning dreams into reality is enthralling!

I am also such a person, so conversations about infinite possibilities with futuristic leaders like Joo Hwee is always a win-win. Both of us would become indescribably excited as the creative energy is sparked and we feed off each other's positive vibes, inspired to immerse in optimistic dreams of the bright future ahead.

Joo Hwee's mind would constantly sprout new, bright ideas. Once lit, it was hard to switch off. Once he figured out the direction, he would intuitively begin conceptualizing the major pieces, working out the next steps and then thinking about who the best person on his team to deploy. Much like a massive turning wheel whose momentum builds and soon, the wheel gains enough energy and speed to sustain its movement. Once it reaches that point, it would take more energy to stop the wheel from turning, than to keep it going.

During one of our conversations, Joo Hwee, in his usual way, excitedly wanted to unpack his brilliant plans and bounce ideas off me. Then he shared a thought: 'I spoke to my team last week about my tentative direction. They were not as excited as I had hoped. I understand their concerns, as they are managing a full plate now, but I think we should just push through this initial period. It's just one more thing. It's going to hard but I believe it will be worth it. These opportunities are too precious to be missed and we will be in a much better position than we were before,' he said, with a certain level of resolve on his face, indicating that he was quite determined to convince his team and get them to take up the new project because it was 'just one more'.

But is it really just one more? What does
taking on 'just one more' truly entail?

Speaking from past experience, there was a time that a certain hunger drove me to push myself forward, too. Like Joo Hwee, once I saw opportunities and possibilities, the fear of missing out on them was far greater than the fear of having to deal with the extra workload that came with taking them on.

Here is reality and the hard truth, one that all of us at some point in our lives need to find courage to face. Every opportunity we encounter at first seems small and insignificant, somewhat like a seed. Each tiny seed is full of potential, waiting for the right conditions for it to begin sprouting. As the seed grows, its mass would increase, resulting in a to-do list that fills up more rapidly than it can be cleared. What seems like a naively simple idea at first, begins to snowball and increase in size until it eventually turns into a mighty giant ball of work.

We know what it takes to perfectly operationalize an idea into reality. The devil is in the details. As the list of other activities required to continue nurturing the seed of an idea grows in size and complexity, we begin to fatigue. But because we have already put in so much, the seed—now a seedling—we feel it's too wasteful to give up and hit pause. So, despite the heaviness in our bones and dreariness in our souls, we persist on, with just one more.

'It's only one tiny item on the list.' 'Ah, there, maybe another one too.' 'Oh, before I forget, here's another to add on.' 'Theoretically speaking, with proper planning and resource allocation, all will be well.'

In reality, the amount of focused, sustained effort required to nurture a seed of an idea to eventually give birth to a giant tree, is undeniably hefty. We need to be honest with ourselves and to our people, and admit what taking on 'just one more' really means.

Earning a living can be stressful, and we need to ensure there is life left to live after earning it. Getting 'just one more' done is achievable but we also must ensure the sacrifice we make is not one we will live to regret.

In workplaces, the responsibility to manage increasing demands and pressure is often left to the employees themselves. But in my opinion, creating workplaces where work is loveable and life is liveable, is the shared responsibility of both employees and decision-makers.

Leaders can continue to hold the mindset of: 'It's just a little more effort.' 'It won't take much. My people are talented and capable and can be stretched.' 'All it takes is for the team to manage their time better.' 'Perhaps a mindfulness programme will help them focus better and work faster.'

Essentially, this thinking stems from an erroneous assumption that the resources are unlimited. We know resources are anything but unlimited. Life itself is finite but most young people hardly consider the notion of mortality unless they have first-hand experience of death and loss.

So there is joy in possibility. There is excitement in potential. There are boundless opportunities out there for the taking, but we also need to be honest with ourselves.

If life and resources were a box of matches, there is a limited number of matches available. Some resources can be replenished, some cannot. That simply is a reality of life. So as we pursue our ideals of a life of unlimited potential where the sky is the limit, we also need to choose wisely and invest our resources—matches—strategically.

My question to Joo Hwee then was, 'I get it, there are so many opportunities out there. I also recognize your team is feeling the weight and have raised their concerns because they want to do well, not because they are shying away from more work. So I'm wondering, if your resources were matches and the opportunities were bonfires, and you are now only left with one single match, which bonfire would you choose to light?'

Joo Hwee thought about it and I could almost hear the gears in his head turning—he nodded as he got the answer he needed.

'Be realistic about challenges on the ground' was the top competency people selected for managers to navigate changes, selected by 78.7 per cent of respondents in the Leaders People Love Global Survey.

Self-Evaluation

- How do you evaluate if your team should start something new or not?
- How honest are you about what it really takes to turn an idea into reality?
- What are the capabilities you need to support your team to acquire in order to become successful in the endeavour?
- While there is fear of missing out, is there also joy of missing out?
- As you pursue goals and achievements, how will you determine if the sacrifices are acceptable to you?

Your Reflections

How do you evaluate if your team should start something new or not?
How honest are you about what it really takes to turn an idea into reality?
What are the capabilities you need to support your team to acquire in order to become successful in the endeavour?
While there is fear of missing out, is there also joy of missing out?
As you pursue goals and achievements, how will you determine if the sacrifices are acceptable to you?

22.6. Have Your Marigolds and Rose Bushes in Place

Imagine yourself juggling lumps of hot coal. The franticness and frenzy can be easily imagined. The heat from the coal as it slaps your palm and you hurriedly toss it back into the air before it scalds you permanently—when work feels like that, how would you react?

Some people think this is a case of poor prioritization and might suggest using the Eisenhower Decision Matrix to prioritize and sieve through the tasks one is supposed to do. This way of prioritization is not a new tool and many people are familiar with it.

This tool basically splits tasks into four quadrants:

Urgent and Important	Urgent and Unimportant
Non-urgent and Important	Non-urgent and Unimportant

Based on which quadrant the tasks fall under, you can take the recommended actions: do it immediately, dedicate time later, delegate or delete the task.

Some leaders I meet have frantic hands juggling many lumps of hot coal. They come with a whole different set of challenges. Though high-functioning and highly capable, they struggle to 'keep it together' and were stuck in a permanently reactive mode.

Their issue is not a lack of prioritization, willpower, or capability to resolve their issues, but teams being overwhelmed by the incessant volume of issues in the pipeline demanding their attention, that they have no mental capacity to prioritize at all.

In other words, it's not an issue of executive skills (time management, prioritization) but an issue with the lack of marigolds and rose bushes.

Allow me to explain.

Some years ago, I visited a vineyard and the hosts took us on a tour on a buggy. As we went around, we noticed beautiful rose bushes at the end of a row of vines. These were aesthetically pleasing and we had a very good time learning about the art of winery.

The guide was explaining to us how climate and other environmental factors affected the taste and quality of wine. While I cannot remember the scientific specifics, the gist of what I got was the usual—keep the bugs away, keep the mildew and bacteria away, get the temperature right, etc.

Someone then remarked at how beautiful the rose bushes were and asked the guide if the vineyard sold roses too.

She chuckled and explained, 'Oh no, that's not why we have the rose bushes at the end of the rows. You see, having healthy vines is the key to high-quality grapes that eventually lead to superior wine taste and texture. To keep them healthy, we need to know if there is something in the air potentially harming their health. Roses are susceptible to many fungal diseases like black rot and mildew, and they also attract bugs like aphids. So our gardeners check the health of the rose bushes regularly, for it will indicate early signs of threat. Once we detect the threat, we can mitigate the risks to the vines.'

Similarly, marigolds are planted around gardens to control the population of harmful pests typically found in gardens. In addition, marigolds also eliminate toxins found in plants, increasing the health of the garden.

Both plants serve the same purpose—an early warning system.

So back to the issue about highly capable people struggling to keep it together—it's not just about making sure a problem is solved quickly, but also ensuring that the pipeline is kept clean. Only the issues that most deserve your team's attention must enter it.

In some organizations, I have observed that even the littlest matters are escalated. Due to the size and complexity of the organization and being in the thick of the action, they don't immediately see patterns. Being deep in the system, sometimes inheriting certain job functions, also blind them to what was 'normal'. But to a neutral outsider like me, it sounded anything but normal. To make matters worse, many of the critical issues fell into the same patterns and their root causes could have been addressed much earlier—if only someone had the bandwidth to look into those recurring issues.

A constantly frantic workplace is the best way
to destroy motivation, productivity, and results.

That's why strategic leaders need to put rose bushes and marigolds in place. These are your early detection systems that identify matters that would only require a little amount of focused attention to prevent them from escalating into crises. With early warning, threats can be promptly negated. Over time, the reactive mood of the office will slowly change into a proactive and responsive one.

Some questions I asked Joo Hwee to help him uncover the patterns were:

- How can everything be urgent and important?
- Why are there are so many burning issues?
- How do cases get escalated?
- What patterns are there among the critical cases? How can we identify the same patterns and put some rose bushes or marigolds in place, before matters turn critical?

If we did not address the issue of the overflowing pipeline, then no matter how fast the team worked, they would eventually be underwater. Joo Hwee needed to act fast as there was only so much someone could handle—any of it could serve as the last straw that broke the camel's back.

With this understanding, Joo Hwee quickly took action. By our next meeting, he had discussed with his team some rose bushes and marigolds—early detection mechanisms—and adjusted the criteria for escalation, decentralizing the decision-making on certain matters to better manage the pipeline.

22.7. Deconstruct the Steps to Excellence

'What you permit, you promote. What you allow, you encourage. What you condone, you own. What you tolerate, you deserve.'

Unknown

Many senior leaders feel burdened by the endless rounds of vetting slides, papers, reports. Certain vetting processes can take up to ten rounds before perfection is finally achieved.

That's a gross amount of man-hours—time that nobody in this day and age can afford to squander on repetitive, low-value work, because these hours are far better spent on other more meaningful and high-value work (remember highest-yielding activities from 22.3.).

Their question would then be: How could they cut down on the number of vetting rounds while not compromising quality, so they could spend their time on better things?

My key questions for them every time were:

- Why would someone get something wrong so many times?
- Are they given what they need to succeed?
- What's the root cause—knowledge or experience gaps, or a mismatch between the dispositions needed and what you have?

In my experience, a few things could cause people to repeatedly make the same mistakes:

1. Too many layers of approval, where each layer has their own mind about what they want, causing multiple changes to trickle down the line. When someone at the start of the report changes something, another thing dependent on it at the end may not align.

2. An overwhelming volume of (paper)work breeds undisciplined thought.
3. Kicking the can down the street because people might assume somebody else would vet and pick up the errors further down the line.

For an organization to be excellent, we can explore the potential benefits of switching the mindset from 'seeking approval', to getting every member to be committed and accountable. To achieve this, I recommend adopting a mindset where matters are 'pre-approved'.

Adopting a mindset where matters are 'pre-approved' does not mean things are allowed to run rogue. It means one works to equip their teams with a solid understanding of why they do the work they do, and what they need to achieve. When people exercise good judgement and discernment, excellence will happen.

How you respond when you receive a sub-par piece of work often makes a difference. Similar to how you first respond to a new idea makes or breaks psychological safety (see 8.1.), it could erode or build psychological safety.

Ultimately, what you permit, you promote.

Key Points in a Snapshot

* Busyness is not importance. Activity is not productivity. Effort is not contribution.
* To maximize your results, everyone must invest in their highest-yielding activity.

Self-Evaluation

* How can you elevate your team's work from operational to strategic?
* How can you assess if your team is involved in their 'highest-yielding' activity?
* When you provide feedback, how can you balance between focusing on details (e.g. dotting the i's and crossing the t's), or on the broad, strategic perspective?
* Do you currently observe a 'kicking the can down the road' syndrome in your team? How can you stop people from kicking the can or passing the buck?

Your Reflections

How can you elevate your team's work from operational to strategic?
How can you assess if your team is involved in their 'highest-yielding' activity?
When you provide feedback, how can you balance between focusing on details (e.g. dotting the i's and crossing the t's), or on the broad, strategic perspective?
Do you currently observe a 'kicking the can down the road' syndrome in your team? How can you stop people from kicking the can or passing the buck?

23

Theme VIII: Mastering Stakeholder Management

*The art of leadership requires you to influence effectively
and turn stakeholders into your best partners.*

As leaders grow in their careers and expand their influence, they begin to realize that stakeholder management is crucial. It often makes all the difference between frictionless collaboration and antagonistic cooperation. For the rank and file, misalignment at the top often creates uncomfortable tensions that result in deadlocks or power struggles.

Stakeholders, however, do not only include those at the top. A stakeholder is anyone who has a stake in your success, so it includes everyone within your 360 remit. Your stakeholders are people from whom you need to have a buy-in, so you can attain a frictionless state of collaboration.

When agreements and *aha!* moments outnumber confrontations and disagreements in your day-to-day interactions, work will become enjoyable. As you develop this important aspect of leadership, consider how you can seek to understand the needs and objectives of stakeholders, manage their expectations, and effectively communicate with them in order to reach a common goal. Effective management of stakeholders will involve identifying and prioritizing them, and addressing their interests while ensuring that the organization's goals are met.

Leaders must understand how to engage stakeholders in meaningful dialogue to build trust and ensure that they are fully apprised of developments within the organization. This helps create a supportive environment where people feel valued and their opinions are heard. In addition, stakeholder management can help leaders effectively manage resources, identify potential risks or issues before they become problems, and allocate resources for new projects or initiatives.

Effective stakeholder management is essential for any successful leader as it helps create opportunities for collaboration and success while mitigating risks. By engaging with stakeholders on a regular basis and building strong relationships with them, leaders can strengthen their organizations and develop trust-based partnerships with those who have a vested interest in its success.

23.1. Compound Your Currency to Enable Change

Some people prefer to sit in an office in their little corners, doing desk-bound work. Others are drawn by the excitement of being in the thick of the action—they would rather immerse themselves when exciting things are unfolding than watch from the periphery.

I once believed that as long as I did my work well, someone—anyone—would notice and recognize me for my hard work, dedication, and loyalty. It took me five years to realize that in workplaces where stakeholders are everywhere, getting your work done and being hardworking is a basic, not a bonus.

Five years passed, and all I did was warm my seat and abuse my already-overused keyboard. I missed out on my first promotion precisely due to this. Spending five years doing my work properly and zealously, I neglected the most important currency needed to enable change—relationships with stakeholders. The worst news for me was that I had lost so much time.

Relationships are like money; when invested in the right place, they give results. Many realized too late that their badge of diligence and dedication is worth little without relationships. Think of this like a bank transaction. Every move you make requires you to have some currency in your balance and if you don't even have an account with the bank, then no transaction—no matter how small or big—would be possible.

Consider the level of your currency. Do you have enough to ask for change?

Here is a typical scenario.

At times, simple things become massively difficult because the stakeholders are not on board.

At those junctions, all we need is a senior leader or someone who can pick up the phone and remove the barrier for us. It could be calling in a favour, explaining things in a way that makes sense to the other person, or simply requesting someone to do something out of goodwill, even if it means inconveniencing them a little. People with whom we already have relationships—currency—would reveal their helpful side easily.

'Your network is your net worth' is a line that we frequently hear repeated among senior leaders. That's also why, I believe, many people take executive education seriously—not because the curriculum is the most important, but because the network and relationships are often the enablers of change.

Navigating Joo Hwee's Conundrum

In Joo Hwee's case, his team was in an awkward situation where they were poking their noses into many departments, ruffling many feathers and as a result, his team got stuck very often. This doused their drive and motivation as they often felt helpless and frustrated.

There was a particularly difficult department. Every request for information was met with resistance and evasion, and after months of trying, his team was close to giving up. Joo Hwee came to our session wanting to work on motivating his team. I had other ideas.

'What is the real problem, Joo Hwee? Based on what you have told me about what your team is trying to accomplish, they all sound like very reasonable asks,' I enquired, truly curious when something seems simple yet is anything but simple.

'Why . . . I'm not sure. I don't know my counterpart so I don't have a good assessment of their true motivations,' Joo Hwee replied.

That is precisely the issue—lack of understanding of the stakeholders.

Agile Leadership Pointers

Understanding your audience is the foundation of your influence.

Your best bet at bridging a gap is to truly, deeply understand your audience. Oftentimes, this is the true cause of resistance and lack of alignment. In a world where there are many ways to go about a problem, it's usually less about the solution itself than about the currency you have—or in Joo Hwee's case—do not have.

As he was not even familiar with his counterpart in the other department, there was likely not enough mutual understanding between them about each other's objectives, intentions and thinking processes.

Even if the solution makes perfect sense, if there is not enough goodwill and familiarity to compel the other party to want to help you, then every request you make would be seen as just more work—and people these days do not appreciate getting more work.

My encouragement to Joo Hwee was to make that first move and break the ice with his counterpart so that his team could begin to move the stones that would eventually turn into mountains.

23.2. Articulate Your Value Clearly

'I just feel like that is taking us for granted. It's almost like we are the garbage can, taking on everything that people don't want, and them turning around to blame us!' Charles grumbled.

Charles was an operations manager whose team was put together to handle 'special projects'. Issues that did not fit into any department's scope but needed to be done anyway, would go to them.

When the team was first set up, Charles was excited by this opportunity. He felt like the team leader of an elite special task force. Understanding the complexity of the issues they had to disentangle and set in order, he took time to handpick the members of his team. Each was known for their ability to solve problems in the face of uncertainty and to thrive under pressure.

Things started off fine. Then slowly, he realized more and more projects were being labelled 'special'. They rapidly reached their bandwidth and started drowning. To make matters worse, his team was frequently grilled and put in tough positions, getting hauled up to answer for the follow-up deliverables and results. That was not what Charles had signed up for.

The agreement, as Charles understood it, was that his team was to be involved in demystifying anything new, work out the process, and then after working out the structure and assigning the responsibilities, go on to work on other special projects. However, it seemed like people had misunderstood and instead, passed any unwanted job on to them, including the ownership of deliverables.

'What is the difference between being the garbage can and the elite special task force?' I asked.

'Well, we are a group of people with very unique skills. When given something is new and unclear, we are able to analyse what is needed and then match the right capabilities with the deliverables needed, while deeply understanding what other departments can do,' Charles explained.

'It's clear to me where your responsibilities begin and end. It's also clear what type of "mess" requires your expertise. But it looks like your internal customers are not clear. What do you think?' I asked.

This is a problem I'm seeing across many organizations. The issue is more severe in those that are actively transforming, usually those on agile journeys. At times, even departments that have been around for a long time face this problem.

People come and go. Leaders who instituted the guiding principles or processes also come and go. When there is a lack of continuity and too many moving parts, the rationale behind past decisions can get lost in translation and misunderstandings consequently arise.

That's also why 'lack of alignment' was cited as the top barrier to innovation in large companies by 55 per cent of respondents in a survey conducted by Innovation Leader, an online resource for corporate innovation teams (Kirsner 2018).

To increase alignment, articulate the value you bring so that others understand how they can work together with you efficiently and effectively.

23.3. Don't Boil the Ocean

Agility is not about being the fastest to react.
It's about responding in a way that will help matters instead of making them worse.

Driven leaders often want to be a catalyst for change. They want change done faster and better, but alas, things don't always go according to their wishes. Sometimes, despite the best intentions and thorough, detailed planning, things just don't pan out the way they were supposed to. Whenever this happens, there's frustration.

Instead of turning up the heat and trying to boil the ocean, the wiser response would be to take a pause, step back and re-evaluate:

- Is the timing ripe?
- Are the people in the right seat, in the right bus?
- Are the key stakeholders and partners in place?

Instead of feeling frustrated, exercise patience. Conserve your energy and resources, and chip away at the issue gradually. When the time is ripe, all resistance will melt away and that little bit of 'strategic boiling' will show its results.

Agile Leadership Pointers

Have patience to play the long game.

Key Points in a Snapshot

- Misalignment starts at the top. Address it so the working levels can collaborate frictionlessly.
- Understand what motivates your audience so you can strive for win-win outcomes.
- Establish a clear understanding about what value you bring and how you should collaborate.
- Be patient and wait for the best timing.

Self-Evaluation

- What comes first for you—tasks or people?
- What's the state of your influence and currency to ask for change?
- Who are your stakeholders? How can you begin to build/strengthen your relationships with them?

Your Reflections

What comes first for you—tasks or people?
What's the state of your influence and currency to ask for change?
Who are your stakeholders? How can you begin to build/strengthen your relationships with them?

24

Joo Hwee's Outcome

Working on the Strategist was a key focus in my work with Joo Hwee.

Highly strategic and respected in his organization, Joo Hwee's insights were always appreciated. In the past, he saw this as an indication of his value and how much he was appreciated by the organization, but lately, he was experiencing a sense of burden as his scope and involvement continued to grow. He also started yearning to immerse himself in other areas of learning necessary for the organization's future. His schedule became so full that he hardly had time to reflect or learn new things.

Like a hamster on a wheel, his life was spinning out of control. Joo Hwee had a niggling feeling that he was not as focused on the future as he should be.

One of the first intentions he expressed was to maximize his resources and talents. That included investing his time and attention into the right things—future, strategic areas, emerging fields, and also talents under his charge. He realized that as their leader, he had been the invisible lid, unknowingly promoting certain behaviours that did not add value, for it caused them to remain status quo instead of being stretched further.

A significant moment we had in our work together was when Joo Hwee proudly said he had cut his meeting time by 30 per cent, without compromising quality. This helped him free up time so he could focus on his highest-yielding activities.

He first noticed that people were not always fully prepared or clear about what they needed to get out of the meetings they held, and that often caused meetings to overrun, spilling into other activities, which then pushed the real work into the evenings. By strategically limiting the amount of time available to meet as a group and scoping the conversation clearly, people began to realize that attention and energy indeed were precious, finite resources, and regard it as such. As a result, as the level of thoughtful preparation increased, people started communicating more accurately, collaborated beforehand proactively whenever possible, asked better questions to seek his guidance more effectively, and only surfaced to him the issues that needed his particular attention.

Consequently, the entire team became more productive and engaged, resulting in shorter meetings. For his team, the shorter and more productive meetings brought back some joy and sense of momentum. Joo Hwee was also able to find time to immerse himself in cutting-edge technologies, finding renewed joy in his work.

THE VISIONARY

INSPIRING COLLECTIVE ACTION TOWARDS
A COMPELLING FUTURE

One of my children's favourite character was Thomas the Tank Engine. Although I found many episodes rather boring, I watched nearly the entire series with my children. Of the many episodes I had seen, a particular one is etched in my mind, even though more than a decade has passed.

Thomas was running down a track with his coaches, Annie and Clarabel. Soon, the day turned bad and Thomas, at the head of the train, noticed an adversity. 'Bust my buffers! No more tracks ahead!' yelled Thomas.

What would you do if you were Thomas? For context, Thomas the Tank Engine is unable to reverse himself. It looked like Thomas had no choice but to brake and stop, but he did anything but that. He quickly hollered and tapped on Annie and Clarabel for their assistance. They removed the train tracks from behind them and passed them forward so Thomas could lay the tracks as they inched forward.

Just like that, Thomas and the coaches arrived at their destination.

Isn't that how leading an organization can feel like today?

When train tracks run out, it's far more important to keep your team together, 'lay the tracks as you travel' and inch toward your goal.

25

Why the Visionary Is a Leader People Love

The Visionary understands that great things can be achieved not just by individuals singly, but by a group, collectively. Valuing the group and the collective over the individual, the Visionary's strategic focus rests on bringing as many team members on board as possible, with a compelling story.

The Visionary strives not to convince everyone in the group of their vision, but to attract the right people to join the collective. Expecting 100 per cent conversion is near-impossible. The Visionary's mission and duty is to communicate in a way that connects ideals and attracts the right people, who find the intended vision meaningful. To a Visionary, it's expected that some people will feel the vision is not for them, which is quite alright. A visionary leader would rather provide adequate information so people can consciously choose to follow a vision which does speak to them. This, too, is one way to help people find meaning and purpose.

To ensure they attract the right team to pursue the vision, this leader individualizes and tailors the message to align with people's needs, and communicates using a flexible range of methods. Storytelling is hence a core competency for the Visionary. For leaders to be masterful storytellers, they need to be excellent listeners as well. So the Visionary pays attention to voices from the ground to weave a compelling narrative that ultimately inspires actionable steps to reach the goal.

Refer to https://leaderspeoplelove.com/resources
for more tools and strategies.

25.1. Guidelines for the Visionary's Storytelling

1. Do your stories inspire confidence by
    a. indicating the general direction forward? Or
    b. reminding people of the unchanging mission or values?
2. Do your stories show your authenticity by
    a. divulging your vulnerabilities strategically or sharing common sentiments?
    b. renewing your commitment to support people?
3. Do your stories connect logically by
    a. laying out necessary facts that lead to a common understanding?
    b. sharing the criteria of your decision-making or evaluation so that people can make choices for themselves?
4. Do your stories build trust by
    a. keeping people in the loop about matters that involve them?
    b. sharing what you do or do not know?
    c. committing to doing what is right for people and for the organization?

26

Meet Jay

An Advocate for Change and Transformation

'We have sent out emails, clarified matters more than once at the town hall, and still, people are asking the same questions, again and again!'

Exasperated and at his wit's end, Jay's voice rose as he shared his frustrations about the situation at his organization.

Feeling like he had tried everything possible to accelerate change and large-scale transformation, Jay was desperate for a solution. To make matters worse, he was deeply frustrated to hear about various factions of people resisting the change, making things chaotic and discordant.

This was quite the opposite of the frictionless experience he had imagined. The leaders working directly under him were having an equally tough time, busy rectifying courses of action, defusing quarrels and correcting misalignment. Although they had supposedly discussed and agreed upon the goals and necessary course of action, most things were not progressing according to plan.

The employees were asking all sorts of questions:

- 'We used to do this. Now we are being asked to take on that. So what's going to happen to what we used to do?'
- 'That department is supposed to do this. Why is it our responsibility now?'
- 'You guys keep piling on more and more work. How are we supposed to cope with the additional headcount?'
- 'Why is there another restructuring? When will this end?'

Like Jay, many leaders I have supported since 2020 are in a similar position. Traumatized by the COVID-19 fallout, many companies engaged in restructuring to keep their businesses relevant and responsive to hostile market conditions. But to the people on the ground, these changes felt like wave after crashing wave that threatened to drag them under.

Some resilient ones strove to make sense of new goals, new roles and furiously paddled to stay afloat. But being in a constant state of flux for extended periods can wear down even the grittiest, hardiest souls. Not to forget, major change often riles tempers and increases tensions at work.

Jay's strategic plan to transform and elevate the organization felt as flimsy as a house of cards—easily toppled by a puff of air.

I often think of managers at the top as conductors. To make music, a conductor has to draw the music out of his musicians—all masters at their respective instruments—superbly. Though they are unified by a musical score, it's his guidance and interpretation of the music at the moment that enables the musicians to coordinate, complement and blend their sounds to create a beautiful performance collectively.

It's often the same in the context of work. The leader needs to 'conduct' his team to draw out their best, creating a beautiful outcome. But when a plan is not well-executed and all the moving parts go in different directions, it results in chaos, frustration and stress. What would it take for Jay to align his teams as perfectly as possible? That was what we needed to figure out.

27

Theme IX: Making Work Purposeful and Meaningful

> 'I am a human being, not a human doing.'
>
> Kurt Vonnegut, American writer and humorist

Purposeful and meaningful work is important as it provides one with a sense of fulfilment. Joy and increased motivation result from us feeling appreciated for contributing to something greater than ourselves. Meaningful work allows us to tap into our passions, use our strengths and contribute positively to our world. Additionally, it can create a sense of belonging within teams and help build meaningful connections between people who share similar goals and objectives. Ultimately, by engaging in purposeful and meaningful work, we can bring greater value to society while finding personal satisfaction in our endeavours.

The fundamentals for living a meaningful life are a healthy sense of belonging, identity and purpose—all of which work can provide. According to McKinsey & Company's extensive research (Bromley et al 2021) over the past three decades, Americans have put an immense amount of value into finding meaning in their work—more so than income or job security. A staggering 70 per cent indicated that work was their sole source of purposefulness. This is also congruent with Gallup's research on well-being, according to which, career well-being was often found to be the most important aspect of a person's overall well-being (Clifton and Harter 2021). Given the positive associations between purpose and meaning and total well-being, making work meaningful is hence not a 'nice to have' but a 'need to have'.

The business-related case for healthy workplaces and organizational leaders is strong. Happier employees are correlated with higher levels of engagement and productivity, and consequently, profitability. Some researchers argue that all jobs can have meaning, but what constitutes meaningful work is subjective. How can we then make work meaningful?

To understand the constructs of what makes work meaningful, I refer to Victor Frankl's work in logotherapy, a 'therapeutic approach that helps people find personal meaning in life', to uncover the possible avenues of meaningful and purposeful work.

1. **Deriving meaning through creation values.** That is, through what we create, achieve, and accomplish.
2. **Deriving meaning through experiential values.** That is, through what we see and experience as human beings, be it by immersing ourselves in nature, feeling like a part of a whole or feeling connected with the larger universe.
3. **Deriving meaning through attitudinal values.** This is achieved by exercising our choice to find meaning even in the most non-meaningful situations, or when suffering and our struggles seem pointless, simply by shifting our attitudes.

    A fourth avenue was named by Kenjiro Uemura, a student at the Graduate School of The Open University of Japan in 2018, which is:
4. **Deriving meaning by having meaningful relationships or being part of a collective group of people.**

Based on these four possible ways of creating meaningful life (and work), the following section will suggest the ways by which you can increase the sense of meaning and purpose in a workplace by unpacking the vision of the organization in a variety of ways, thereby strengthening the Visionary within you.

Key Points in a Snapshot

- 70 per cent of Americans indicated in a survey that work was their sole source of purpose.
- Meaningful work is an important part of a fulfilling life and sense of well-being (Source: Gallup).
- What constitutes meaningful and purposeful work varies, with four possible avenues you can explore.

27.1. Understand Your Audience Thoroughly

My book *8 Paradoxes of Leadership Agility* (2020) discusses the paradoxes commonly faced by leaders. Some readers indicated in their interaction with me that they identified with certain paradoxes more than with others. The paradox 'Executing vs. Inspiring' resonated with many.

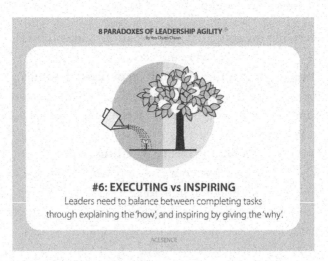

The question often on leaders' minds is: 'When the speed of implementation and go-to-market are crucial, should I just get people to execute the vision (i.e. simply instruct them and expect them to follow orders) or help them enjoy what they are doing by inspiring them and helping them see the goals at the end?'

Not every leader is comfortable playing the inspirational role. I can understand why. It requires time and effort, and much consideration. However, a powerful vision can be communicated in simple ways, if you understand what motivates and compels your people to act. The ultimate purpose of this communication is to rally your forces behind the vision and motivate them to act collectively.

Without this outcome, the communication would not have attained its goal. That would be like having the world's best product without any buyers. In the context of leadership, you may have the best plan in the world, but if no one is following or executing it, it's as good as any bad plan.

Most leaders I meet do have the idea that they need to strike a balance between executing and inspiring. Based on their professional training or preconceived models, they usually either place too much emphasis on the goal, or focus too much on the steps to get there. In the next sections, I'll share more on why both of these are issues and how you can manage them better.

'Leadership is the capacity to translate vision into reality.'

Warren Bennis, scholar, organizational consultant, and author

---

Focusing Too Much on the Big Goal

You may already be familiar with this idea from Stephen Covey's *The 7 Habits of Highly Effective People* (2013): to 'Begin With the End in Mind'.

To apply this, you first envision the end and then work backwards to create a plan, and then with discipline, check the steps off one by one. This excellent habit has many benefits and I have personally reaped good dividends by applying it to reach my own developmental milestones. This was how I managed to pivot my career from teacher to executive coach and business consultant, with a thriving business, within a few short years. I always had the larger vision in mind while working towards the next small goal. Luck had very little to do with the outcome.

Most people, however, focus only on the first half of this high-performance habit (envisioning) and gloss over the second half (an executable plan).

> 'The problem isn't that people think too big; it's that they fail to plan big.'
>
> Brendon Burchard, high-performance coach

Having a big, audacious dream is not enough to carry everyone forward. This is the first common mistake I see senior leaders making. They rehearse for hours to deliver a compelling speech that speaks only about the big, audacious dream. On certain occasions, we can use this approach (like at major annual kick-offs, while setting a general direction), but at other times, when we need people to start taking actions that are new and unfamiliar, a dream alone is not enough.

But what exactly do they need? The answer to this varies across the board, as:

- Some people are excited by the dream and feel 'the bigger, the better', while others may feel deflated by a dream that feels overwhelming and unattainable.
- Some may be distressed if left alone to 'figure things out' for themselves, as the reality of bringing about change can often be messy and unstructured. Others may be thrilled to break new ground and navigate uncharted waters.

The Leaders People Love Global Survey sheds some light on how people view changes, and their managers' abilities to navigate these changes. Participants were asked to rate:

- the level of disruption faced in their workplaces;
- the manager's readiness to navigate change;
- competencies that managers need in order to navigate change better.

Nearly 61.8 per cent of respondents said they face 'very high' levels of disruption in their jobs, and only 27.6 per cent of respondents rated their managers' ability to navigate changes as 'very effective'. The top competency that nearly 78.7 per cent of respondents picked as one of their top choices, was 'be realistic about changes on the ground'.

This is why some people 'fondly' describe their managers as people living in ivory towers, detached from realities on the ground. This corresponds to the common pain points I hear from high-performing leaders who feel sandwiched between expectations from the top and struggles on the ground.

Recall the earlier theme about creating human-centred workplaces. In the current volatile times, it's unwise for leaders to ignore concerns and push through resistance. It may work for a short time but once trust is broken and with a persistent lack of empathy, leaders would lose the currency to demand any kind of change (See 23.1.)

While we must strive to have every last man on board to pivot and change, focusing too much on the end and ignoring current challenges can create unintended consequences. Middle managers, often playing the role of bridges and facilitators, could be left with a gaping divide too difficult to bridge, if they too feel overwhelmed. This would create further misalignment down the line.

What can you do then?

Balance your approach between inspiring and executing. As you strive to inspire, offer your people solutions to overcome their current challenges, so they can see a way forward. You can acknowledge that you are aware of the reality on the ground and then offer some insights or reframes, so they can start removing barriers and put the plan into action. Instead of leaning only towards inspiring, use both ends of the paradox suitably.

Focusing Too Much on the Implementation

The other spectrum of issues arises when leaders try to navigate the paradox, 'Executing vs. Inspiring' by leaning too far on the side of executing. These leaders tend to be detail-oriented and prize perfect implementation above all else. Instead of getting people to understand the rationale behind a vision, they focus all their energies on getting every single step of the implementation right.

I can understand why they do this. That's the purpose of a well-thought-out plan, isn't it?

Here's a joke that has been making rounds online with slight variations. It's about a seemingly nonsensical act of guarding a bench. Here's how it goes:

Guard the Bench

A newly appointed camp commander noticed that one of the duties given to soldiers was to guard a bench around the clock. At the appointed time, two soldiers would appear, stand on both ends of the bench, and their mission would be to prevent anyone from sitting on it.

How strange! Why would anyone put a bench in an open area yet disallow anyone from sitting on it! Curious, the camp commander goes over to investigate. He wanted to understand the rationale behind this 'senseless' duty. Upon further queries, the commander got even more confused. He was met with 'We don't know' and 'some sort of tradition' and 'we didn't ask', which made the commander feel even more baffled.

'This makes no sense! I have to get to the bottom of the matter!' he thought to himself.

His persistence paid off. He found the previous commander of the camp. One after another, he went up the chain of command, at last locating the first commander, a 100-year-old retired General who had held command of the camp some sixty years ago.

The response from the centenarian was: 'What?! You mean the paint still hasn't dried?'

This highly likely fictional story illustrates how important it is for teams to understand the 'why' behind the actions, so that they can evade irrelevance.

In the real world, this is a typical situation where separate teams work on connected tasks without knowing how they all fit together in the larger scheme of things. It's a classic case of 'the right hand doesn't know what the left hand is doing'. As a result, efforts may be uncoordinated and poorly synchronised, although the end goals are the same. This is not unlike rowing a boat where both the rowers are not synchronised—the boat will keep going in circles and get nowhere.

As the member of a team many years ago, I can recall quite a few incidents when my team and I were tasked to carry out certain actions but were not told the rationale behind the actions. Having a gap of understanding made me feel very annoyed, for the approach we were tasked to adopt seemed highly inefficient. We were trudging along half-heartedly, dealing with internal resistance, going in circles with little to show for our efforts. We were creating our own self-fulfilling prophecy, with the task destined to fail because of our half-hearted efforts.

One day, I couldn't stand being left in the dark any longer and went to my manager for some answers. It was only when she explained that I finally understood the rationale. Like a light bulb that had switched on, everything finally made perfect sense! This made me more willing to accommodate inconveniences while executing the plan because I fully understood and bought into the larger strategy.

Some people might be inclined to label managers who withhold information as 'sly' or 'power hungry' but I highly recommend adopting a more neutral and empathetic approach. I can recall a particular junior manager who intentionally focused only on the plans and steps. Even though he was bombarded with multiple questions from people demanding to know the rationale behind every change, he shared only sparingly. When asked why he had chosen such an approach instead of unpacking the intent and thinking behind the broad strategy, he responded: 'I think it's best to simplify the message because knowing too much of what goes behind the scenes might overwhelm people. I prefer not to burden them with the difficult decisions and uncertainties we are still dealing with. If they know the full picture, I'm afraid it would seed even more fear and anxiety because honestly speaking, the plan's next part isn't clear yet. It's better not to bog them down with additional information.' This junior manager's intention in withholding information was to shield his team from additional anxiety.

In certain contexts, this way of thinking has some value. We might communicate parts of the original intent on a need-to-know basis. Leaders have to understand when the situation warrants that kind of response. Herein lies the complexity of being an agile leader and becoming a leader people love.

Agile Leadership Pointers

Involving people appropriately as the plan takes shape increases commitment and alignment.

A Balanced Approach

What you communicate should depend on what will motivate the team.

Eventually, the purpose of a compelling vision is to inspire shared action. The ability to bring people to a common understanding and be adequately motivated to carry out a vision is a key success indicator of a leader today. It's far less about how smart the leader is, than about how good the leader is at inspiring others to take action. Getting others to move and take the right actions is a better measure of success. Otherwise, it will simply be 'all talk and no action'.

When the 'why' behind the steps is unclear, the people on the ground might find their work meaningless. They might also not feel excited or challenged enough to strive toward the goal when the rationale behind the strategy is unclear. When leaders focus too much on the steps and neglect to adequately educate people about the goal and its intent, the well-thought-out strategy loses its value and is reduced to mindless actions, much like asking the soldiers to guard a bench.

What can you do then?

Balance between executing and inspiring

As you strive to inspire people to take the right actions in the right spirit, offer them what they need. This requires you to first understand what they need to be convinced that the strategy, as well as the implementation plan make sense. Some may need to know the 'whys', or the thinking and evaluation criteria and how the plan was formulated. Next, offer resolutions about the next steps, acknowledging the difficulties and telling them how you can support them as they plug the new plans into existing processes. Use both ends of the paradox in your communication.

What is the right balance between executing and inspiring, you may ask? It all depends on your audience, so take the time to get to know them well. Your effectiveness as a leader lies not only in casting a compelling vision but also in inspiring *shared actions*.

Key Points in a Snapshot

Different people are motivated by different things. Some want clarity about the next steps and the immediate future; others want the bigger picture and to know the 'why'.

Self-Evaluation

- When communicating, what is your preference? Big picture or detailed steps?
- How much do you understand about the mental capacity of your team? How much uncertainty or complexity can they cope with?
- What do you know about what motivates them? Clear plans or clear why?
- What is their current level of understanding, and what else do they need to know so they will move towards the goal?
- Given that there is no one-size-fits-all, how can you collect 'intel' by asking better questions and then craft better stories?

Your Reflections

When communicating, what is your preference? Big picture or detailed steps?
How much do you understand about the mental capacity of your team? How much uncertainty or complexity can they cope with?
What do you know about what motivates them? Clear plans or clear why?
What is their current level of understanding, and what else do they need to know so they will move towards the goal?
Given that there is no one-size-fits-all, how can you collect 'intel' by asking better questions and then craft better stories?

27.2. Ominous Outcomes Are Not Inspiring

I was sipping my favourite coffee while having a conversation with Jay about how he planned to give an inspiring speech the following week.

"'Now that we have finally met the first milestone, we have to work even harder to increase our market share. We need to look at our processes. That means everyone needs to now go into the last detail of our processes to make sure everything is aligned. That might mean you have to put in longer hours. The work is going to be hard, but there's no choice." That's what I'm going to tell them tomorrow. I hope it will inspire them.'

I choked on the coffee and nearly spat it out. Why the big reaction?

In 2011, Bronnie Ware, an Australian nurse who spent several years in palliative care, wrote a book titled *The Top Five Regrets of the Dying*, which were as follows:

1. 'I wish I'd had the courage to live a life true to myself, not the life others expected of me.'
2. 'I wish I hadn't worked so hard.'
3. 'I wish I'd had the courage to express my feelings.'
4. 'I wish I had stayed in touch with my friends.'
5. 'I wish that I had let myself be happier.'

Notice that 'I wished I had worked more' did not make the list. If you check out the list of 'top new year resolutions', I am certain 'working more' will not make that list either.

To be honest, of the hundreds of leaders with whom I have worked in close partnerships—every one of them driven and dynamic—not a single one has ever confessed that they want to work more. Agreeing to 'work more' and 'work harder' is a politically correct statement we say only to people who want to hear it—to our bosses, maybe.

To inspire their teams, leaders would do well to be more honest and accept that 'working more' is not going to rank high on being motivating and inspiring. Though people are still likely to work hard, shape the narrative in a way that ignites fires. People are not afraid of hard work but of meaningless work.

It all depends on the point of view from which you construct the narrative. When you shine a light on the right ideas, you inspire people.

Highlight the wrong parts and you will demotivate them instead. Such is the art of communication and persuasion.

Agile Leadership Pointers

Shine light on the right ideas to ignite fires of motivation, not douse them.

Visionary leaders consider how the mind and heart would perceive an upcoming experience. The perception can be a weight or a catalyst depending on how it's contextualized even while the goal remains the same, and what needs to be done may not change.

Some ways you can communicate better are:

- Zero in on the emotional benefit. Building on what makes life meaningful and purposeful, you can consider the following angles:
  o The accomplishment benefits not only the collective but the individual
  o The experience of doing something worthy together
  o The higher meaning behind working hard
  o The relationships and collaborating with colleagues
- Focus less on the actual process of what needs to be done. What needs to be done is usually the easy part once motivation is in place. When something feels too big or tedious, it creates an internal barrier within your people. To be persuasive, you will need to work to lower this barrier.
- Do not hide the truth about how much work is needed, nor the magnitude of matters. Simply shine a light on what makes the work meaningful; make that the focus so it raises motivation.

Navigating Jay's Conundrum

I challenged Jay to relook at his 'inspiring' speech and consider it from the listener's perspective. That required him to go beyond what was politically correct and look right into the hearts of people. He realized the issue with the narrative he was painting and reworded it to the following:

'When all this is over, we will be well-positioned to increase our market share. We have all worked very hard to get here, so what we need to do next is to keep up our momentum and maximize the outcomes while minimizing our effort. That means we want to make sure every little effort we put in translates into a large yield. To get there, we are going to do away with everything that is irrelevant or low-yielding. The road will be tough—this is where I need your help to work together and filter through all our processes so we can maximize our outcome and minimize our effort.'

As we conclude this section, I know this view might not sit well with you. I met a senior leader (my boss) who got angry when I suggested we should not be asking people to do work increasingly hard. Her retort was, 'How can you even suggest that people should work less hard?'

I understand that within a system where all activities are skewed to increase productivity and profitability for the sake of a healthy GDP, leaders feel they cannot say such things. But here's the unpopular view:

- Working hard is a given.
- We glamourize hard work or the hustle culture excessively and prize it over accomplishment.
- Greater accomplishment is often rewarded with further uphill ascent.

Perhaps it is time to explore another perspective because:

- the tides are turning.
- employees are changing.
- they are demanding total well-being.
- the hustle culture is not sustainable.
- hard work will be a part of our lives for a long time, but leaders can make hard work feel lighter, more meaningful and more purposeful.

Self-Evaluation

- How can you adapt your communication and make work more meaningful and sound less ominous?
- What is the effect of work on your people? Positive or negative?

Your Reflections

How can you adapt your communication and make work more meaningful and sound less ominous?

What is the effect of work on your people? Positive or negative?

27.3. What's in it for You?

'I just promoted her, gave her a substantial increment, and now she wants to leave?' Leaders used to fly into a rage when they learned that their high performers had decided to leave the organization.

Understandably, the loss is significant. Being highly responsible, accountable, and committed, they tend to be the pillars of their respective work teams. Due to the positive energy these high performers bring to the workplace daily, their decision to move on to other pastures (not necessarily greener) may come as a shock.

Some leaders take such news personally, feeling a sense of betrayal, or as if they were misled. Others respond with self-blame or pure confusion, wondering what they may have done wrong, or what else they could have done to retain the talent.

During the global pandemic, it seemed that many high performers left their organizations, sending shockwaves rippling through the system, destabilizing already shaky organizations. An article by McKinsey about The Great Attrition reported that only 35 per cent of workers who left their jobs between April 2020 and April 2022 returned to jobs in the same industry (Smet et al 2022). This means it became increasingly challenging to replace the vacant position with someone having similar experience and skills. Against the backdrop of shrinking talent pools, the exit of high performers is a problem worth examining.

When your high performers leave you despite appearing engaged, responsible, accountable, and committed, something bigger may be at play. Leaders need to unearth the real causes to prevent history from repeating itself.

Jay faced a similar situation. I took the chance to help him analyse and understand it. In his mind, he had done everything right and had seen no warning signs. I gently reminded him of Step One of the Re4 Model, 'Reconstruct the Map'. Jay then decided to make full use of the exit interview from before his high performer left. Some questions he wanted to have answered were:

- Was there something he could have done?
- What can he learn from this experience to better understand his team's needs and aspirations?
- If a person seemed motivated and engaged but still wants to leave, what else could be missing?

As expected, Jay found good insights from his conversation. Here was what his team member said:

'I get the mission and the importance of the work. I was challenged and grew a lot. Each stretch task came with a considerable amount of discomfort and I always asked myself, "what was all that for?" Other than the growth, was the struggle to keep up with the workload worth anything at the end? After a while, I couldn't find the answer. It slowly came to a point where I was only surviving on my sense of responsibility. It seemed like I was operating out of habit to deliver but I felt less and less joy. Ultimately, I kept pushing myself because I did not want to let others down. I always want to give my best.

'My moment of decision came when I realized I was not sure what was meaningful to me. While the mission is important and benefits many people, it's not my mission. I want to spend time now exploring other options and find what is meaningful to me.'

When leading teams, it is easy to focus on the gaps and neglect the people who seem to be 'doing fine'. In Jay's case, he had assumed that high performance and engagement were sufficient indicators that someone found purpose and meaning in their work. If Jay had not made that assumption and had instead spent time to uncover what was purposeful and meaningful to his high performer, he might have noticed the misalignment earlier on and taken corrective action.

Note to reader: Since my work with Jay revolved around other themes, I have excluded his overall outcomes from here.

Key Points in a Snapshot

- High-performers could be burning out in secret, so watch out for them.
- Positive work performance might not be an indicator of purpose and meaning.

Self-Evaluation

- What occupies the majority of your discussions? Work or personal interpretations of work?
- How can you weave in topics of purpose and meaning into your work discussions?
- How do you know if the work you do is meaningful and purposeful?
- What can you do to make the work you do more meaningful and purposeful?

Your Reflections

What occupies the majority of your discussions? Work or personal interpretations of work?
How can you weave in topics of purpose and meaning into your work discussions?
How do you know if the work you do is meaningful and purposeful?
What can you do to make the work you do more meaningful and purposeful?

28

Meet Olivia

A Manager Tasked to Head a New Department

'I have been asked to lead the new department after the restructuring but I'm not sure if I should take it on,' said Olivia apprehensively.

I was curious. Having worked together for a while, I knew Olivia had been seeking opportunities to elevate her career. Leading a new department with a brand-new scope sounded like just the kind of opportunity she had been waiting for, so I had to ask what was holding her back.

'Honestly, I have never felt like my manager truly cared about me and the success of my career, so for her to suddenly be so enthusiastic about offering me this opportunity has made me suspicious. Is it really an opportunity or a chance for her to get rid of me?'

The success of any new strategy relies heavily on how well it was unpacked and fleshed out. We needed to first overcome Olivia's doubts, before getting her team on board.

29

Theme X: Inspiring Trust

'Trust is the lubrication that makes it possible for organizations to work.'

Warren Benni, scholar, organizational consultant, and author

What is leadership without trust?

If you don't trust the person standing in front of you, imploring you to follow the direction and charge ahead, would you do it? The most likely answer is 'no'. It does not really matter how compelling the story is, if you have no trust in the storyteller.

Research has shown that trust in leaders and teammates are positively correlated with engagement at work. In the Global State of Workplace 2020 survey conducted by ADP Research Institute (Dr Hayes et al 2020) spanning across twenty-five countries, trust was found to be highly important in workplaces. The research defined trust at three levels:

1. Trust teammates to do what they say they will do.
2. Trust my leader.
3. Trust the senior management of my organization.

People who rated 'strongly agree' in just two of these levels of trust were found to be three times more engaged, whereas those who checked all three levels were found to be fifteen times more likely to be fully engaged.

We all know in our heads that trust in one's leaders is the foundation. Without trust, one doesn't have even the most basic of all social currency to propose the way forward and beseech others to follow them. This is why the findings from McKinsey's report in 2021 (Dondi et al 2021) are so alarming. Education levels and the competency 'inspiring trust' are negatively correlated, meaning the more highly educated a person is, the lower is their ability to inspire trust.

When I first posted about this result on LinkedIn, it was met with more agreement than not, but it also invited some strong objections from a couple of people—you guessed it, they all happened to be quite highly educated. They questioned the validity of this survey. Given that the survey covered 18,000 people across fifteen countries, I would take a second look at it before dismissing it as 'untrue' or 'made-up'. Sometimes, the truth can be a tough pill to swallow.

I don't think any leader sets out with the goal to breed mistrust, but it happens anyway. What has gone wrong?

I refer here to the Trust Triangle devised by Francis Frei and Anne Morriss (2020). According to this, there are three drivers of trust: authenticity, logic and empathy, which are defined as follows:

- **Authenticity:** I experience the real you.
- **Logic:** I know you can do it; your reasoning and judgement are sound.
- **Empathy:** I believe you care about me and my success.

When trust is absent, one of these drivers is broken.

In my experience, it's usually either authenticity or empathy that is broken. The difficulty is rarely with logic because, in many of our educational experiences, logic, truth and facts are highly prized. Logic, being measurable and tangible, is also how leaders often tend to build their case and strengthen their argument to persuade and influence. Over the years, I have met leaders who are superior in logical and analytical thinking, but years of overreliance on logical thinking has dampened their abilities to show empathy and authenticity.

Maybe we have been hardwired to be logical but now is the time to change, because when authenticity and empathy are broken, the effects can be damaging. Without trust in your leadership, little can be accomplished.

We see evidence of this in the Leaders People Love Global Survey. Among respondents who rated themselves as 'happy at work', close to 35.6 per cent picked 'cares about me as a person' as one of the behaviours exhibited by good managers. Multiple reports on the most important leadership skills have also rated empathy as a top requirement.

To fulfil one of three drivers of trust, authenticity, it's important for you as a leader to know yourself first, and be guided by your own values on your leadership journey. (See Chapter 2, 'Construct Your Leadership Map' for more. See Daniel's story in Chapter 10, and 8.2. 'Trust as a Leadership Brand'.)

In the following pages, I am going to show you how you can strengthen the Visionary in you and improve your ability to inspire trust, especially when things are uncertain, volatile, and complex.

29.1. Keep People in the Light, Not in the Dark

'We know the restructuring exercise is on the way but we have no clarity yet. I have tried asking my manager—he is as clueless as I am. Honestly, the feeling is hard to bear. What am I to tell people? Would they think that this is a sinking ship? Will they still have a job? What would the change mean for the work we do now? It's so hard,' said Olivia, worry creasing her forehead as she heaved a sigh of helplessness.

Not surprisingly, the senior management had taken a long time to work through the restructuring, keeping everyone in the dark. Only

Olivia knew she would be heading a new department overseeing a new scope, but that was about all.

Within senior management, a storm of activities was unfolding as they did their best to predict the best possible direction for the organization and the optimal new structure to move forward. But from the outside, the people only saw a vacuum of knowledge with the only update being: change is coming. They received no further updates from senior management until two months later.

The long wait and lack of updates had done their damage by then. Being kept in the dark made people anxious, suspicious and uncertain. By the time the announcement finally came, the entire organization's morale was in shreds. People's motivation to carry out their day-to-day duties had waned; their drive for existing initiatives had plummeted as many started searching for other jobs, just in case, to ensure they would have stability, as their confidence in the company was flailing desperately.

This is a classic example of how organizations manage change poorly. I always give this reminder to leaders with whom I work:

Agile Leadership Pointers

Keep people in the light, not in the dark.

People naturally imagine the worst when dealing with the unknown.

Change is the only constant and an abundance of research has been conducted on how change should be managed. According to a report by Gartner in 2020, organizations today have, on average, gone through 'five major firmwide changes in the past three years—and nearly 75 per cent expect to increase the types of major change initiatives they will undertake in the next three years'. This was before the emergence of COVID-19 globally, so we can expect the rate of change to have increased tremendously since.

Due to the perennial challenges businesses face, managing organizational change became one of the hottest topics in the conversations I have had with leaders. Many of them tell me that change is always difficult; they expect resistance, as humans are creatures of habit. I used to think like that too, but one day, I realized that I was being held back by this self-limiting belief.

In the Global State of the Workplace 2020 by ADP Research Institute (Dr Hayes et al 2020), the team set out to discover the connection between workplace resilience (ability to navigate change) and engagement. As 2020 was also the year that the entire world was affected by COVID-19, the researchers had expected workplace resilience of the employees in a country to be directly correlated with the impact of the pandemic in the country (average cases per million, average deaths per million and unemployment rate). However, the findings indicated the following few surprising results:

- The degrees of impact of COVID-19 on a country had no effect on workplace resilience.
- Individuals who were personally affected by COVID-19 demonstrated much higher levels of workplace resilience.
- Workplace resilience increases with more workplace changes. In particular, employees who experienced 'at least five changes at work were 13.2 times more likely to be highly resilient'.
- People who enjoyed what they were doing at work were 3.9 times more likely to be highly resilient.

The research also found the following surprising results around trust and resilience:

- People who trusted their managers, their teammates, and/or senior management strongly, were forty-two times more likely to be highly resilient.
- When senior leaders are transparent and forthcoming in sharing information that individuals need to know before they need to know it, keeping them prepared, resilience levels tended to be higher.

Behaviours that are congruent with being transparent and forthcoming include:

- Inducing confidence in people by keeping their focus on what would remain unchanged, despite the volatility.
- Offering sufficient resolution, telling stories 'with drama, detail and dialogue' as they take people forward with confidence, instead of fear of the unknown.
- Leading the way forward by conquering small, attainable steps and supporting their teams along the way as they inch forward.

The greatest conclusion from this research was: The more changes there are, the more resilient people become.

> 'When stressed, we catastrophize . . . When we get stressed or feel out of control, we shift down to our primitive coping mechanisms, ramping up our fear responses and shutting off the prefrontal cortex. The higher the levels of arousal or stress, the stronger those primitive circuits get, the less affected you feel by things that might normally give you pleasure and the more things feel threatening or sad.'
>
> Dr Amy Arnsten, professor of neuroscience
> and psychology at Yale Medical School

Agile Leadership Pointers

Invite peace and self-assurance even when the path is unclear and bumpy.

Self-Evaluation

- How do you keep people informed, giving them a heads-up instead of letting them find out on their own?
- How do you personally feel when you need to communicate changes to your team?
- What will make you feel more comfortable in communicating difficult changes to others?
- When matters are uncertain, how do you regain your sense of peace?
- Who can you seek support from when things are unclear?

Your Reflections

How do you keep people informed, giving them a heads-up instead of letting them find out on their own?
How do you personally feel when you need to communicate changes to your team?
What will make you feel more comfortable in communicating difficult changes to others?
When matters are uncertain, how do you regain your sense of peace?
Who can you seek support from when things are unclear?

29.2. Exercise Wise Transparency

When I work with people, I always encourage them to complete the values exercise. Many of them resonate with value words like honesty and integrity—great values for leaders. As they begin to rise in leadership within their organizations, however, complications arise.

As a member of the senior management team, you would be privy to more information. One of the issues I often encounter is when leaders feel inner conflict about keeping certain information confidential and not sharing it with their team.

This feeling is natural and understandable, but therein lie many dangers if the boundaries are not properly managed. Some pitfalls I have seen are:

- Divulging insider information 'in confidence' to others outside of the circle. This is dangerous as it compromises your trustworthiness.
- Tiptoeing around information that cannot be shared, creating untruths that distract or complicate matters.

How to be transparent yet not overshare is a delicate balance for which there are no fixed rules. Applying your values might be a helpful way for you to manage the tension.

For example, one of my values is honesty, so when people ask me about matters that would infringe on the confidentiality agreement between my clients and I, I might say something like: 'I'm aware of the incident, but the information is not mine to share. I'm more curious about the effects of the incident on you.'

In the workplace, how transparent a leader can be depends on many factors. One size does not fit all here, either. To help you navigate this, consider these questions as you decipher what to share and what to not share:

- How will the information shape people's perception of the leadership team?
- What about how your leadership brand is being perceived?
- What is the real intention behind sharing or not sharing?

- What consequences might there be of sharing or not sharing?
- What value can the listener derive from the additional information? Is it useful or harmful?

29.3. Trust Needs to Trickle to the Ground

'I seriously don't know how to approach this new strategy. Some of it isn't making sense to me either. I can already see so many questions from the ground. Shall I say it this way? Should I not say anything at all?' Olivia was fretting over how to reveal the new strategy to her team as she anticipated strong objections, since the new direction would significantly change some of their job scopes.

The success of every new strategy that emerges depends in part on the communication plan.

> 'A strategic plan must not only stay inside the meeting room.'
>
> An excerpt from Episode 14, *Agile Leaders Conversations* with
> Raymond Tan, Change Coach

The communication plan is usually devised at the senior management level. But often, as the messaging flows through the middle and working levels, its transmission lacks uniformity and congruence. A well-crafted plan simply loses its effect when it gets lost in translation.

Some pitfalls of this that I have observed are:

- **Inconsistency:** The message from the top and middle are at loggerheads, causing confusion on the ground.
- **Ineffectiveness:** Middle managers are unable to unpack the strategy at the working level effectively, causing poor alignment in actions and appreciation of the purpose.
- **Hypocrisy:** When middle managers don't personally agree with the vision and instead take a 'victim' stance that the decision was 'above their pay grade' so everyone, including the middle manager, has no choice but to comply.

- **Arrogance:** Middle managers are not bothered to help the working levels translate strategy into action, asking them to 'just do as they are told', as strategy is not their concern.

Many middle managers, I have observed, struggle to unpack strategies appropriately for their team members at the working level because they feel ill-prepared to do so. Some of the common issues they bring to the conversations include:

- Anxiety as they anticipate strong objections on the ground which they may be unable to handle well.
- Awareness of challenges on the ground, making translation of the strategy into practice impractical and highly abrasive.
- Lack of full buy-in for themselves for they too have doubts and concerns about the feasibility of the proposed plans. Their own managers' inability or reluctance to help them bridge the gap doesn't help matters.

For any strategy to be implemented perfectly, alignment is key. People at the working level will only trust the direction and take synchronized actions when they buy into the vision. It's then not only the responsibility of the top management to craft a compelling communication plan but for the managers to be part of the plan. However, the reality is that middle managers are not always well-prepared to act as effective bridges to bring greater alignment of purpose and fulfilment to their work.

An article published by McKinsey in 2021 (Schaninger et al 2021) found a 70 per cent purpose gap between executives and upper management, and frontline managers and employees who felt that 'they can live their purpose in their day-to-day work'. More alarmingly, nearly half of frontline managers and employees felt they could not find purpose in their day-to-day work. This finding was termed 'purpose hierarchy gap', which further extended to fulfilment in work.

Executives and upper management are 'nearly eight times more likely than other employees to say that their purpose is fulfilled by work'. Looking deeper into the statistics uncovers a more serious issue.

Due to ineffective managerial practices, frontline employees seemed to be conditioned by their leaders to think about work in an un-purposeful way, since they indicated the following trends:

- They were ten times less likely to say that they'd had opportunities to reflect on their personal purpose.
- It was nine times less likely for their managers to 'foster opportunities for them to work on purposeful projects'.
- Managers are not doing enough to 'share the big picture' with frontline employees, resulting in three times less likelihood to see the connection between their day-to-day work and the organization's larger purpose.

The last thing an organization navigating change wants is to have their strategic plans, developed after hours of good thinking, to get lost in translation. This is a gap the Visionary needs to help bridge. To play this role well, prepare yourself to help people at all levels embrace change.

Key Points in a Snapshot

- Keeping people in the loop, especially in times of uncertainty, prevents people from getting stressed and catastrophizing.
- Keeping people informed helps increase trust in leaders.
- There is generally more purpose alignment at the top than on the frontlines. Your middle managers' effectiveness in unpacking strategies makes a difference here.

Navigating Olivia's Conundrum

Returning to Olivia, in helping her to first be at peace with heading the new department overseeing a brand-new scope, I got her to draw up a list of benefits and risks. She also spoke with her manager and a few other senior leaders. Considering her lukewarm relationship with her manager, constructing a fuller picture and understanding of what it takes and what possibilities were available, helped Olivia make an objective decision.

Once she herself was determined to set up the new department on the right foot, ready for success, the next phase of our work was related to the communication plan.

As part of the new department, Olivia had 'inherited' some team members who were performing various functions. The change impacted each of them to varying degrees, so she needed to give them more assurance and clarity about the road ahead. Here was how I helped Olivia prepare.

For her team:

- Anticipate objections from the ground and prepare the answers.
- Be clear about what can be disclosed and how, and how much.
- Explicitly make connections between day-to-day work and the big picture.
- Bring people to an understanding about what will change and why, and what will remain the same.
- Set up cadence for regular updates for two-way communication.

To further her own understanding of the new strategy and what it will take to actualize it:

- Check her own buy-in and understanding of the new strategic direction. When in doubt, gain a better understanding by discussing with peers or other senior leaders.
- Set up a schedule with stakeholders to discuss issues that require more discovery and alignment.
- If doubts cannot be cleared, demonstrate support for the direction in the present moment and treat the upcoming phase as an opportunity to collect useful evidence to feed forward into a better strategy in the future.

Note to reader: Since my work with Olivia revolved around other themes, I have excluded her overall outcomes here.

30

Meet Kiran

A Leader Eager to Prove His Worth

In the following chapters, we will follow the story of Kiran. Kiran was a highly loyal employee who grew rapidly in his organization. He was known to be very effective in driving initiatives. Kiran was excellent with his team and enjoyed a good rapport with his direct manager. He had been looking forward to the next career growth opportunity, hoping for a brand-new role, but due to a perceived lack of 'star quality', his manager did not support his cause.

'Personally, I feel quite ready to take on the next challenge but my manager is not supportive. He said to get to the next level, I need to stop rambling. What a ridiculous comment!' Kiran huffed in frustration. He was fast becoming restless, for he seemed to be doing everything right, yet there was no career growth in sight.

Our work together was focused on helping Kiran discover how he could reverse the way he was being perceived and raise the lid on his progression.

31

Theme XI: Executive Presence, Influence, and Persuasion

One of the top requests I receive from people with whom I work on leadership development, is to raise their executive presence, influence, and become more persuasive. To me, these three are interdependent leadership competencies. On the following pages, I will help you unpack and look at each one with greater clarity.

Executive Presence

'What is executive presence?' I ask.

Most of the leaders stutter or ramble as they try to string words together to explain what they think executive presence meant. They reach for words like 'confidence', 'charisma', 'strategic', and 'gravitas'.

All the above, I think, are accurate ways to describe someone whom we perceive as having executive presence. But is executive presence something we are supposed to have, or be? Is it a skill or an inborn ability?

This is my take: Executive presence is the ability to project authority, credibility, and confidence in interpersonal and public settings.

It comprises both skills and character. Skills-wise, it involves attributes such as effective communication with both large and small audiences in public and private settings. It also includes body language. All these combine to shape a certain perception about you—something we call 'personal branding'. Executive presence has a direct impact on how people perceive the value of what you have to say, your capability to shape direction and lead your organization through both good and bad times.

If we take away the word 'executive', then the following is my favourite definition of what presence means:

Presence [*n*.]: A person's ability to make his or her character known to others.

To me then, executive presence is about character first, then skills. It's more about coming across as confident and trusting yourself before behaving in a way that exudes ease and confidence. Lastly, executive presence is more about gaining the permission and endorsement to lead because of your character, not your title.

I often refrain from defining to my coachees what a leader with executive presence looks like, because I believe this is highly individualistic. I shall not limit their growth and potential with my imagination, but instead, encourage them to get to know themselves better and find the best leadership persona they can adopt.

To me, personally, it's a matter of authenticity and being comfortable in my own skin. It's also being aware of societal expectations and then working with them—not challenging them head-on—as I increase my ease and authenticity. But bear in mind that this is the way I define myself as a leader and how I exhibit my executive presence. I encourage you to determine the same for yourself. (Refer to 2.2. on *Kung Fu Panda*.)

Here are some questions I encourage leaders to consider and revisit as they define what executive presence means to them:

- What is leadership?
- How do your core values shape who you are as a leader?
- What is your reason to lead?

- How do you define your value and worth as a leader?
- How do you lead through tough times? What about good times?
- Why should anyone be led by you?
- Would you be willing to be led by you?
- Why should anyone trust you to do the right thing?
- Why should anyone entrust their careers into your hands?
- When you engage with people, how should they feel?

These questions, along with the Leader of Impact exercise, will help you define and shape your executive presence, so do check the exercise and more resources out on leaderpeoplelove.com/resources

Influence and Persuasion

What are influence and persuasion?

Influence is the ability to shape or change the behaviour or opinion of another person, group, or organization. It can be used in both positive and negative ways, depending on the context and motivation behind it. Influence can be achieved through persuasion, suggestion, bargaining, manipulation, or other forms of communication.

Persuasion is the act of convincing or influencing someone to believe or do something through the use of argument, reasoning, or appeal to emotion. It is often used in marketing, politics, and sales.

Given that I personally lean more towards introversion, I believe I also tend to attract leaders who exude similar energy. Many of them, once we begin to talk about influence and persuasion, appear significantly uncomfortable. To them, the idea of influence and persuasion is closely tied to the idea of selling, which they hate, for they associate 'selling' with being unscrupulous, sales-y and pushy—something not aligned with their values.

But a more helpful reframing is offered in Daniel Pink's book *To Sell Is Human* (2018). Here is a quote I found particularly useful:

> 'To sell well is to convince someone else to part with resources—not to deprive that person, but to leave him better off in the end.'

So what if selling (an idea) is for the betterment of others? Here's another quote I like from the book:

> 'The purpose of a pitch isn't necessarily to move others immediately to adopt your idea. The purpose is to offer something so compelling that it begins a conversation, brings the other person in as a participant, and eventually arrives at an outcome that appeals to both of you.'

What if selling (even the seed of an idea) is a slow-burn process and about conversations that attract others to know more about the new topic, be open about possibilities and then eventually, without any forceful intention, to bring them to a place of common understanding?

With these new ways to reframe influence and persuasion, how will you now approach selling?

Key Points in a Snapshot

- Executive presence is the ability to project authority, credibility, and confidence in interpersonal and public settings. It requires both skills and character, and goes beyond your title.
- Influence and persuasion work on both the mind (logic) and heart (emotions).

31.1. Ramblers and Storytellers

'You know what he did the other day at the townhall? Someone asked a question, I began to answer and I wasn't even halfway through when he tapped my leg under the table and cut me off. I was so embarrassed!' Kiran's ears turned red as he recalled the humiliating experience.

> 'Incessant chatter is not necessarily communication.'
>
> Charlie Kaufmann, *Eternal Sunshine of the Spotless Mind*

Early on in my new career, as I dipped my toes into entrepreneurship, a lesson I quickly learned was, 'A confused buyer will not buy'.

My verbose presentations and pitches caused me to lose one of the biggest business deals of my life. If you had been there, you would have seen how bored the decision-maker was at my rambling and how he was watching the clock as he waited impatiently for me to finally finish. He must have mentally yawned innumerable times.

Like Kiran, I had fallen into the trap of being a rambler. Here are the common beliefs that cause people to be convoluted ramblers instead of persuasive, concise communicators:

- We believe facts add ultimate value to our work and the more knowledgeable we are, the more valuable we are. Every time we are challenged, we believe we should respond with more facts, data and evidence to persuade even the most stubborn of persons. Unknown to ramblers, unfortunately, disagreement or a lack of buy-in is not only an issue of ignorance about facts and data, but a lack of emotional connection.

- We are deeply passionate about our area of expertise and assume that other people should be equally passionate. However, the higher we go, the more our ability to influence others will be tested. We need to master the ability to connect meaningfully with people from other disciplines and areas of expertise. That means being able to **explain things so simply that even a twelve-year-old can understand**. This is the ultimate skill.

Picking up the pieces of my shattered ego after the failed business presentation, I set out to improve my communication skills, particularly speaking more concisely and persuasively. That was when I began to seriously study the skill of storytelling. Influence and persuasion is about sparking conversations and evoking curiosity in people so they look forward to the next conversation. With that understanding, I began to deconstruct the steps that will enable me to stop rambling and start storytelling.

Navigating Kiran's Conundrum

Some key guiding principles I offered to Kiran were:

- It's not about you but the audience—what do they already know, want to know, and need to know?
- Engagement is everything—are you sharing the information in the right way, at the right pace so that the audience is engaged cognitively, emotionally, auditorily, and/or visually?
- Anyone can share the same information—what makes you unique and the best person to do so? How can you share information and convey valuable understanding about you as a leader and person of influence?
- How will you measure success? Define the parameters of every engagement you make—what do you want them to say, feel and do?

With these guidelines in view, Kiran realized that his issue was exactly what had made him successful in the first place—his abundant knowledge.

Being knowledgeable can bring success to you in your career, but those who truly make their mark as senior leaders know how to calibrate their communication—influence and persuasion—with their audience in mind. They stop falling into the trap of being self-oriented, sharing matters that enthuse them but not without thinking about how to tailor the message to suit their audience.

The ability to make a complex idea be understood easily is the highest level of communication. With the right story, you can bring even the most perplexing concepts to life. During organizational transformations, however, we do not see adequate examples of this being practised, for the preferred communication style is primarily logical and fact-based.

Kiran quickly learned to improve his communication and began to see results in double quick time. He used the following questions iteratively to sharpen his communication with his direct manager—his biggest supporter for the role he had in mind:

- What is the objective of the conversation?
- What facts, data, and information are essential?
- What concerns does his manager have and how can they be addressed?
- What resolution or outcomes does he want?
- What would success in this situation look like?

Within a short time, Kiran's manager stopped calling him a 'rambler' and at townhalls, he was able to speak uninterrupted as he made his points succinctly. He felt like he could stand on the stage with the presence he had always wanted.

Storytelling changed my own results too, where I got the chance to recover the deal I lost five years ago—so I encourage you to pick up this transformative leadership skill.

Self-Evaluation

- Do you focus more on what you want to share or what your audience needs to hear?
- How attuned are you to your audience's mental and emotional state?
- How would you describe your current communication effectiveness?
- What needs to be improved?

Check out the Leadership Storytelling course
at leaderspeoplelove.com/resources

Your Reflections

Do you focus more on what you want to share or what your audience needs to hear?
How attuned are you to your audience's mental and emotional state?
How would you describe your current communication effectiveness?
What needs to be improved?

31.2. Listening is the Foundation of Persuasive Communication

Consider the following scenario. Likely, it's a typical one that many would have experienced at home as a child:

'Dinner time!'

Silence.

'Dinner time!'

Again, silence.

'Hey, I said it's dinner time!'

Despite the many repetitions, children would only come scuttling when the parent would lose his or her cool.

This communication pattern indicates that the first instances of speech are likely ignored and in repeating the pattern, listeners are taught (remember: what we permit, we promote) to only pay attention to what was said only when things get heated. The message behind this communication pattern is: what we are saying is unimportant until we lose our cool.

Transpose this scenario to the workplace. A leader who communicates in a similar fashion is also ineffective in capturing the attention of his audience, and hence in influencing them.

Here are some reflection questions for you as a leader:

- As you speak, how effective are you at capturing attention and stopping people in their tracks?
- How often are you able to elevate the quality of discussions, directing the focus towards something more inclusive and productive?
- How effective are you at establishing your credibility as well as trust and compassion as a person of influence?

Now imagine these scenarios:

- You are meeting someone for the very first time, listening intently and then responding with something thoughtful and empathetic, showing your sincere interest in connecting with them.

- At a meeting, you observe and notice conversations going off-track. You guide them back on track, breaking the unproductive chain of dialogue with a well-placed question.
- You make connections between all the diverse viewpoints, shifting perspectives with a powerful question that increases common understanding.

How's that for executive presence and influence? This is where superb listening skills come in. Many people would consider themselves good listeners because they can recall everything that was said. But it is not enough to just hear what was said. Listening goes beyond just collecting information; it involves reading between the lines.

As you listen well, you are really doing the following:

- Hearing what was said.
- Listening for what was not said (reading between the lines).
- Empathizing with the speaker and understanding the motivation behind what was said.
- Connecting, sorting, comparing what was said by various parties.
- Making connections between what was communicated with the topic at hand.

As you begin to listen better, you will also be able to communicate better and then influence more effectively by:

- Asking better questions.
- Summarising key points to improve common understanding.
- Paraphrasing what you have heard to increase clarity in the group.
- Inquiring about irrelevance and discrepancies you noticed.
- Connecting ideas within the group and increasing inclusion.

> *We are born with two ears and one mouth—indicating*
> *the importance of listening twice as much as we speak.*

When you listen well, you will be able to capture attention the moment you speak.

Listening Increases Productivity

Capturing your audience's attention from the moment you begin to speak is efficient and has economic benefits, too. Ineffectively run discussions and meetings result in loss of productivity and creativity.

Research by TED speakers David Grady and Jason Fried in 2014 indicated that eight out of the twenty-three hours executives spend in meetings each week, are unproductive. These were their findings:

- 90 per cent of people report daydreaming in meetings
- 73 per cent admit to multitasking during meetings
- 25 per cent of meeting time was used to discuss irrelevant issues
- 50 per cent of people found meetings unproductive.

To address this issue, you can introduce meaningful stops in a meeting as and when required, gently but firmly bringing people back to the topic on hand. You can also shorten the meeting time, saving many man-hours, freeing people to do the work, increasing productivity.

Certainly, this is a leader people will love.

Listening Elevates Your Value

In an environment where people talk excessively and where society prizes the noisy above the quiet, it can be difficult to remember the value of listening. Swimming against the current can be challenging. Introverts (like me) prefer to lapse into their most comfortable self by staying quiet and just listening, and eventually fading into the background.

But here is the reality.

Staying unknown is the surest way to put a premature stop to an aspiring business plan. An unknown ambition or unspoken aspiration dies before it gets a chance to breathe. Visibility is important for career progression. In my case, I knew I had to overcome my reticence and learn to speak up and show up, because no one was going to buy from a business or person they had never heard about.

> **Reminder:** *No one will notice your good work if you hide behind your computer screen or in your cubicle all the time.*

I do understand the discomfort introverts feel when they are in the limelight. There are days I feel terribly awkward and ill at ease in the midst of more than two strangers.

For those who are introverts like me, there is hope. What I am going to share next will prove useful, regardless of your personality. You can increase your influence, even as an introvert. For ambiverts and extroverts, it will help sharpen your communication as well.

Here's what you can do to elevate your value: The next time someone speaks, listen intently, then paraphrase the key points of what you have heard and extend it further with a good question.

Listening Improves Storytelling

Participants learning storytelling for the first time tend to focus on the words. Working to perfect their sentences, they get carried away trying to craft a message, forgetting that a delightful performance requires not only words, but also presence. As soon as they receive their first feedback from me, they begin to realize that their stories cannot move the audience unless they also exercise another communication skill: listening.

Good listening skills are the foundation of superb storytelling.

A story is compelling only when you understand your audience, using their words like your own; speaking in terms they can relate with.

This means that before you can craft a most compelling story, you must first listen to the chatter on the ground, from the very people you are trying to persuade.

Putting it All Together

Listening, the oft-forgotten communication skill, is also important in elevating the quality of conversations, especially when collaborating with diverse personalities. The purpose of the listener here is to find common ground and use it to build a sense of inclusivity.

Imagine a setting in the workplace where a meeting is underway. The people gathered in this meeting are of various personality types. You have ambiverts, extroverts, introverts, and people from diverse cultures and beliefs, with differing points of view.

As the meeting progresses, some assert their points of view more forcefully, pulling the discussion apart. As a leader, you know you need to step in to restore inclusivity and expand common ground. To regain control and direct the discussion, you need to have been listening to the diverse points of view, and pick the opportune moment to speak up and stop the digression in its tracks. You may even feel as if you have to fight for a chance to air your views. But your ability to capitalize on the slightest pause to inject a helpful thought can change the course of the conversation from one-sided or indulgent, to being more focused and productive. It is simply not enough to speak for the sake of filling the room with the sound of your voice.

What you will say at that moment is essential. Will it capture their attention and focus them on their commonalities instead of differences? Will it cause them to pay attention or to ignore you? This all depends on your superb listening skills.

Key Points in a Snapshot

- To raise your executive presence, be persuasive and compelling; use fewer, better words.
- Stories are persuasive when they touch the heart and connect the mind.
- Great storytellers are great listeners who understand their audience.
- Cultivate superior listening skills, for it increases productivity, improves storytelling and raises your value.

32

Kiran's Outcome

Working on the Visionary was a key focus in my work with Kiran.

Feeling ready for the next step in his career ladder and eager to contribute at a higher level, Kiran was struggling to change the way he was perceived. While he could do his work and lead his team excellently, he was seen as more as a 'high-level doer' and not 'senior enough' to be included among the 'big boys'. His manager was supportive of him but had withheld his sponsorship for Kiran's promotion. Kiran had to get his bosses to buy in and create a new role.

Kiran seemed to have met his Peter's Plateau, the highest possible point of his career at present.

As we began our work to improve Kiran's executive presence, influence and persuasion, the first thing he had to do was to stop rambling. This, he achieved once he switched from a self-centred lens—where he shared what enthused him—to an audience-centred lens. When Kiran focused on what the audience wanted to know, it made them more receptive of him. He was able to hold their attention even while sharing an abstract, highly technical idea because he'd present it in a simple way. With his newfound Visionary skills and attitude, Kiran revisited the topic of his future plans with his manager and how he could contribute at a higher level. His manager was receptive, this time. Eventually, the company created a new position just for him, two levels higher than his current one.

The best part? His manager, who said Kiran was not ready for the next level, became his biggest sponsor and advocate.

33

Meet Maya

A Group Director Who Wants
to Restore Confidence and Stability

'Settled down? They never get to fully settle down from one restructuring before the next one hits them. And now I have to tell them there is another one coming,' said Maya with a tinge of exasperation in her voice.

A group director of marketing and communications at a global medical instruments company, Maya had been going through one restructuring exercise one after another at her company. The one that she brought to our conversations was going to be the fourth one in three years.

I asked her how she personally felt about it, for it would be challenging to help teams make sense of the changes if she could not wrap her own head around it. To my relief, she replied, 'For me, it's honestly okay. I like the changes, actually, and I appreciate why we need them. My concern lies with my team. They seem to be extremely busy. They have no bandwidth to take on more changes. I'm wondering how

I should communicate news of the change in a better way to them this time. Telling them is the easy part—getting them to settle down fully and find a new rhythm is the real challenge.'

Organizational restructurings (or reconfigurations) seem to be the norm nowadays. Like a merry-go-round, people, initiatives and resources are moved around more often than we have been used to. In the past, the word 'restructure' would strike more fear in people than it does today, because it has become so common now. Anecdotally, based on the conversations I have with organizational leaders, it seems as if restructuring occurs as often as every other quarter!

To be perfectly honest, as an observer, I find myself asking the following questions:

- Are the restructurings really necessary?
- How much of the changes from the last round of restructuring exercise have been fully effected?
- Has sufficient evidence been collected to inform the need (or no need) to restructure yet again?
- Even if the reorganizations are experiments, don't we need to let people get the hang of things first, before throwing everything up in the air again? No wonder stress and burnout are on the rise.

According to the Leaders People Love Global Survey, respondents who rated the level of disruption they face at their jobs as 'very high', were asked to select from a list of competencies they believe managers need so that they can help teams navigate change more effectively. From this list, 'unpack strategies and policies clearly' was chosen by nearly 57.1 per cent of the respondents, coming up as the fifth-highest competency deemed desirable.

Maya's assessment of the situation was accurate and congruent with what I have observed—people are generally hardworking and cooperative. But for them to effect change flawlessly, they must be helped to understand the change and how to carry it out. They need help unpacking strategies and policies.

Maya knew her team well. This gave us insights into how to tackle this challenge and create the desired result—to have everyone on board, help them settle into a new rhythm of work and quickly lower tensions within the organization.

Designing an Effective Change Strategy

First, we needed to understand how she approached the communication strategy during the previous three restructuring exercises. I wanted to understand what worked and what didn't work for her team, and explore new ways to strengthen her message, leaning deeply into the Visionary voice.

Here was what we discovered about her communication strategy:

- Factual and highly logical, explaining why the change was needed.
- Informing people of their changed responsibilities.
- Taking questions from the ground.

Maya also noted that most of the feedback she received could be grouped as follows:

- Overwhelming workload, indicating that the change was perceived as 'extra', which might not have been true.
- Disagreements about lines of responsibility creating a lot of tensions, misunderstandings and behaviours that were perceived as 'turf guarding'.
- Losing sight of the greater mission and sense of purpose in the jobs they were tasked to perform.

To help Maya determine a better change strategy, I offered her the following questions. I encourage you to think about them as well:

- What is the nature of restructurings or changes you are tasked to effect throughout the teams? Are they upgrades that improve the overall value or experience, or merely add-ons?

- Think about how you might be subconsciously communicating the ominous nature of the change as being hostile, unfriendly or threatening instead of as an improvement, beneficial and making work easier (refer to 27.2. 'Ominous Outcomes Are Not Inspiring').

- As changes need to eventually trickle down to the last person, we need every team member to be at ease and at peace with the adjustments to their work and scope. To do this better, we definitely need to anticipate the emotions that might be evoked in response to having something taken away. People may feel a sense of loss and worse off due to the change.

- How can you then create a safe space for people to gather, converse and collectively comb through the issues so you can end up with a win-win outcome?

- When their world is destabilized by change and it becomes unrecognizable to them, how can you inject confidence and calm into their psyche?

'I am not lost for I know where I am. But, however, where I am may be lost.'

A.A. Milne, *Winnie the Pooh*

This was an important key. People knew where they were but what this 'where' meant in terms of the big picture, eluded them. It was up to Maya to help them figure it out and to reaffirm that everyone was in the right place.

Maya felt it would help her people to be reminded that despite the organizational changes, their core mission remained the same. With that thought, she knew she needed to tap into her creative mind for a preliminary idea to build an action plan.

34

Theme XII: Activating Change

After crafting a beautiful strategy for change and getting leaders at every level to engage employees with the bigger vision, all that's left is to activate change and bring about the desired transformation.

Change does not happen on its own—it requires a spark in order to gain traction. At times, momentum for change can be created by removing barriers, while at other times, it can be started by simplifying the vision to make it comprehensible at every level. Ultimately, the goal is to create change that lasts. To achieve this and reap the positive outcomes of change, leaders need to activate change that's repeatable and then gets internalized for good.

Research on successful change management, however, is stark. A fifteen-year research from McKinsey has found that 'less than one-third of respondents who had been part of a transformation in the last five years say their companies' transformations have been successful at improving organizational performance and sustaining those improvements over time' (2021).

This is where the Visionary comes in—to spark off a compelling vision and then skilfully maintain momentum.

34.1. The Power of Metaphors

Q: How do you eat an elephant?

A: One bite at a time.

Q: How do you solve a humongous problem?

A: By taking one step at a time.

We all know that 'a picture speaks a thousand words'. This is true not only of tangible, physical pictures, but also of the images in our minds. If we want to encourage someone who is immensely overwhelmed by a monumental task, we could offer sound, logical advice. But this would likely only touch the mind (logic) and exclude the heart.

But associating problem-solving with a mental image of 'eating an elephant' is much more powerful.

First, the mental image evoked can be hilarious and humour works well for grabbing attention. Second, it takes the weight off the issue, drawing out a simple but relevant and transferable solution. Using a powerful metaphor, we outline the need for a cool head and a methodical approach in tackling the huge task.

Navigating Maya's Conundrum

I shared with Maya the power of using metaphors. A month later, we met again. This time, she appeared energetic and cheerful. As I walked into her office, she proudly pointed to a new poster.

'Look, Chuen Chuen! This was what we came up with!'

On the poster was a photo of a red balloon floating in the air and underneath it, a slogan read, 'We tell stories of unsung heroes'. Maya began to share how she improved her communication strategy this time around.

As usual, she laid out the facts, shared the rationale behind the change and addressed concerns. This time, however, she added in a new discussion segment, asking her team this question: amidst all these changes we are all facing together, what remains unchanged?

'We are highly committed to do our best,' said one.

'And also to support one another,' said another.

'Yes, we are a great team and I'm thankful for that. What else remains unchanged?' Maya asked in an attempt to peel back the layers even more.

'Our work? Our clients? Who we serve?' said one.

'It's our mission to tell stories that float like balloons . . .' said another.

And there it was, the metaphor that captured Maya's attention, eventually resulting in the poster with the red balloon.

Self-Evaluation

- Do you explore other ways of communicating to achieve greater impact?
- Going beyond facts and logic, what other faculties of the mind can you engage?
- The human brain does not think in letters and words but in images, textures, and colours. How can you strengthen your communication effectiveness by tapping into the natural way the human brain works?

Your Reflections

Do you explore other ways of communicating to achieve greater impact?

Going beyond facts and logic, what other faculties of the mind can you engage?

The human brain does not think in letters and words but in images, textures, and colours. How can you strengthen your communication effectiveness by tapping into the natural way the human brain works?

34.2. Keep Inching Forward

'Wow, the meeting earlier was so inspiring!' exclaimed my colleague. 'Yes! I was feeling quite down with a bout of the Monday blues but now I'm pumped!' said another. 'So what are we supposed to do? Was there some follow-up to this new project we are embarking on?' I had to ask. Both colleagues gave a silent shrug.

Have you ever been in a meeting where you felt hugely inspired only to leave and wonder what you needed to do next? Was the meeting only for information? Good to know? How clear was the follow-up action plan and by when you needed to act?

The Leaders People Love Global Survey indicates that one of the top wants of respondents was for their leader to give them better clarity and sense of direction. For respondents who rated themselves as 'happy at work', around 32.5 per cent selected this as one of the contributing factors to their happiness. Similarly, for respondents who rated themselves as 'unhappy at work', around 46.3 per cent of respondents chose 'lack of transparency and clarity of direction' as a behaviour missing from their workplaces.

When navigating through a series of changes, getting people to buy into the vision is the first step. The next step is for them to see the bigger picture and find meaning in their day-to-day work. Once you have achieved alignment in direction, the next step is to ensure movement. After you have given the awe-inspiring speech to stir people, you need to activate change by getting them to take action. This completes the process of inspiring change.

To activate change and bring about movement, you can provide:

- Clear timelines
- Next steps
- Next milestone

You did your part to ignite the spark so far. Now it is time to get people moving.

34.3. Lubricating the Climb

'Things are so tough now! Every day I go to work and I feel so burdened. This migration is so tedious that any mistakes would be disastrous. I don't know how much longer I can do this. Maybe by the end of all this, my hair would all turn white!' I recalled how one of my coachees, Jody, exclaimed with exasperation, once.

I can empathize with her sentiments. Some work saps our energy, while other refills our tank. Every role will have a mix of work we enjoy, that we feel neutral about and that which recharges us. For Jody, this system migration requires hours of meticulous work, which she found draining, unfortunately. There was no one to whom she could delegate this, as the entire team was needed.

Knowing there was no easy way to avoid this work, I asked her, 'Given that this tough period will continue for a little longer than we both would like, and knowing that this work will cause a lot of heartache, headache, turning your hair white etc. . . . at the end of it all, when you look back at this years later, what will make this feel worthwhile?'

Jody pondered for a moment then burst out laughing.

'All our hair turning white together! What a scene, the whole team with white hair!'

Just like that, a difficult upward climb felt easier. When the work gets tough, who better to do it with than with your friends at work?

In the Leaders People Love Global Survey, 52.5 per cent of respondents named having 'work friends' as one of the factors that increased their happiness at work (respondents could pick as many factors as they liked from a given list).

While some may argue that colleagues cannot become genuine friends, I believe professional relationships can be supportive and mutually beneficial too. Instead of expecting people to leave their personal lives at the door and 'be professional', think about how you as the leader can create conditions for goodwill and collaboration.

Whether people move forward to become real friends or not, the key is to create the space where they can enjoy the company of people they work with. Work will then become more productive and satisfying.

A study by the University of Pennsylvania and University of Minnesota found that close friendship is positively correlated with productivity (Jehn et al 1997) as work friends tend to communicate better. They encourage one another and are more committed to helping one another.

When I look back at my career, I too find corresponding experiences. The years where I worked among a team of friends, we achieved many important goals, and overcame obstacles together. Our will to thrive and succeed together was high. Till today, those years are the highlight of my time in the workforce as part of a team.

This is also aligned with the fourth construct of meaning and purpose by Kenjiro Uemura, 'deriving meaning by having meaningful relationships or being part of a collective group of people'.

Key Points in a Snapshot

- Sustaining change permanently is equally, if not more important, than starting the change itself.
- Seek various ways to sustain momentum. Tap into your understanding of the team.
- Compound small steps into big results.

Self-Evaluation

- What is your natural style as a leader? Task- or people-focused?
- How can you make completing work as well as building relationships a part of your routine as a people leader?
- With hybrid and flexible work arrangements, what practices can you introduce so that work friendships are formed organically?
- What is your self-help mechanism when the going gets tough?

Your Reflections

What is your natural style as a leader? Task- or people-focused?
How can you make completing work as well as building relationships a part of your routine as a people leader?
With hybrid and flexible work arrangements, what practices can you introduce so that work friendships are formed organically?
What is your self-help mechanism when the going gets tough?

35

Maya's Outcome

Working on the Visionary was a key focus area in my work with Maya.

Handling wave after wave of restructuring, Maya's team was having a hard time keeping up. Tensions were rising as their job roles began to overlap (turf guarding) and the lack of clarity resulted in additional work—or so it was perceived. She needed to help them get out of the chaotic environment, the senseless running about without appreciating the mission they were really fulfilling.

The first thing Maya did was to align them once again with their unchanging mission. Their mission was to tell inspiring stories and make their organization's great work accessible to the public. This drove home once again that everyone was on the right bus and in the right seat. The exercise of creating the metaphor carrying shared meaning proved to be far more effective than we had both expected.

In the past, when she had tried to facilitate 'streamlining' work, some people would get defensive and refused to let go of their work. After the red balloon metaphor, people began to think differently.

As they looked at their overflowing plate of responsibilities, they also became aware that some missions are better accomplished by working together as a team. That meant the best person with the right skills and scope would take it up. The delineating of overlaps was rapidly sorted out, workload on the whole reduced without compromising results.

At our final session, Maya looked very relaxed and at ease. Her team was in good shape. Spirits were up, morale was high.

As I asked her for a final closing reflection, she said, 'This is the first time we have settled down and internalized the change. Now that I know what needs to be done, we are ready for the future.'

THE AGILIST

EMBRACING AN EVOLUTIONARY WAY TO LEAD WITH RELEVANCE

> Success is sometimes the outcome of a whole string of failures.
>
> Vincent van Gogh

In our lifetimes, we often taste the bitterness of failures before the sweetness of success. We might look at others deemed 'more successful', 'more effective' and wish we could be as 'lucky' as them, but I don't believe in overnight success. Instead, I opine that all the successes we witness are the results of 'failing forward' (a phrase popularized by Dr John C. Maxwell).

Failures are unavoidable, but failing consistently is preventable.

In my first career as a math teacher, I remember frequently referring to a poem by Portia Nelson, titled 'Autobiography in Five Chapters'. This poem speaks about the importance of first taking responsibility for one's failed endeavours and then forging a different path. But as the poem illustrates, we might be tempted to repeat our actions. After all, we are creatures of habit. To succeed, then, we need to go against our nature—to always observe, review, evaluate and then measure our effectiveness. Only by constantly being curious about the connection between our actions and outcomes, can we predictably shorten the string of failures and achieve timely success.

36

Why the Agilist Is a Leader People Love

The Agilist values learning from their past experiences and acts with intention. With a futuristic lens, leaders who are Agilists leverage the effect of high-performance habits compounded over time to continuously upgrade their skill set, elevate their mindset, and thereby improve their results.

Relevance is top-of-mind for the Agilist. This inner voice embodies the principles of agile leadership—the ability to lead and navigate complexities with a sense of authenticity and ease. The Agilist is changing and constant at the same time, and is well aware that the risks of remaining unchanged far outweigh the risks of moving forward and making mistakes.

The Agilist is an avid learner and curious about the world. Knowing results can be either limited or liberated by the depth of one's perspective, the Agilist appreciates opportunities to interact with people who are different and is eager to view the world through their lens so employing a new, updated lens may be possible.

The Agilist uses the Re4 Model as a constant guide, and frequently revisits the steps:

- Reconstruct the Map to discover what has changed and become irrelevant.
- Refresh the Lens to understand why old assumptions need to be challenged and updated.
- Renew the Identity to feel sure of the role you need to be play in upcoming endeavours.
- Rebuild the Capabilities to gain the most vital skills and attitude which will extend your relevance.

Refer to https://leaderspeoplelove.com/resources
for more tools and strategies to increase your agility.

37

Theme XIII: Leading with Relevance

> 'There is always something more to learn. Even for a master.'
>
> Master Oogway, *Kung Fu Panda*

Many leaders I work with are short on time. With boundless responsibilities strapped onto them, they carry the weight of the world on their shoulders. Many of them, led by moral values and principled living, are aware that their every decision has far-reaching impact beyond just the bottom line and organizational lifespan. They understand that what is at stake are the lives (and livelihoods) of people with whom they interact daily at work.

Will the people become greater as a result of their interaction and learning? Or will they be diminished and be in a far less advantageous position due to the trials and challenges that befall them? It all depends on the judgement of their leader.

I can understand the pressure. But the way in which we push ourselves as leaders is not effective. It results in a broken system.

When more is required of us, our instincts put us in the fight-or-flight mode. We habitually exert ourselves more, push every single muscle in our bodies to work faster, and push harder. This way of working is unsustainable. If we don't elevate our perspectives, we will be trapped in this vicious cycle—resulting in broken bodies, broken souls and spirits.

The leaders I work with don't lack the capability nor the willingness to give their all. They have pushed themselves to reach one milestone after another, but despite their best intentions and abilities, the issue that eventually diminishes their results is irrelevance.

I have met many leaders who continued to repeat actions that were no longer effective. Trapped in their own antiquated views, they were blind to that fact. Despite their best efforts, they had fossilized in their ways, unable to move forward.

To guard against irrelevance, we need to ask ourselves:

- Have we put in place processes that alert us when we are off-course?
- Have we surrounded ourselves with people who would offer alternative perspectives that widen our perspectives?
- Have we continuously grown and adopted the mindset of the lifelong student, constantly checking our relevance?

Relevance in leadership is the ability to understand and relate to the needs, values and beliefs of those being led. Leaders must be able to recognize current trends, changes in their environment and workforce, and be aware of the issues that are important to the employees of today. This can mean understanding market dynamics, staying up-to-date with industry news, or even recognizing cultural shifts within an organization.

Relevant leaders are aware of the big picture—they remain ever-ready to adapt their strategies to changing circumstances. By staying updated about topics and trends, leaders are better able to motivate their teams and help them reach common goals.

A leader needs to be relevant in order to lead effectively. To forego relevance is a folly.

In the following pages, I will offer some exercises that you can consider to increase your relevance and develop the skills and attitudes that will help you be more agile and effective.

37.1. Your Life in One Line

In 2012, after suffering a series of career setbacks, marred with relationship issues on both professional and personal fronts, I decided enough was enough—I had to correct the trajectory of my life. I had gotten stuck and remained there for far too long.

By chance, I came across a personal leadership development programme led by Dr John C. Maxwell. Over the course of a year, via an online university, I studied his leadership teachings. The programme culminated in a convention in Orlando, Florida to celebrate our graduation from the course.

This programme, very reflective in nature, offered many opportunities for me to re-examine my values, purpose, and meaningful contributions to the world. It also shaped my approach towards human capital and leadership development. I realized that we, as humans, in general, tend to expend too much energy on taking on more and complicating matters. But in times of turmoil and confusion, what we need most is to simplify and declutter. This seems counter-intuitive in our busy worlds, but is necessary.

Simplifying does not mean minimizing our problems or denying their complexity. It simply means removing distractions so we can focus on the core and the heart of the matter.

This thinking was further enhanced as I continued my learning as an educator. One of the curriculum design models I underwent trained us to ask 'why', 'what' and 'how' recursively until we arrived at the one understanding that would endure through time.

Agile Leadership Pointers

All the actions that guide you in work and life are based on an enduring theme that is consistent throughout your life.

In John Maxwell's programme, we were tasked to summarise our life. I have variations of this exercise where participants were asked to write their eulogies. In my religion, eulogies are not common so that was not something I resonated with. But John's assignment was both daunting and exciting.

The task was to write one line that summarized our life. (We were given a word limit as this line was supposed to be one that could be carved into a tombstone.)

I took many days to ponder, reflect and then decide on that one line that could define my life.

I wrote many sentences, all of which sounded outstanding. Then reduced them to phrases, then single words until I had found mine—only two words. (If you want to know what my line was, please email me.) It was difficult to do because all the words that made the final cut were inspiring.

But the hard work was worth it. I changed as a result of the disciplined exercise. It helped me see clearly what my life would be about (and conversely, what it would not be about). It helped me pare down and purify the activities I embarked on and guided my decisions from thereon.

Agile Leadership Pointers

Your agility is relative to your ideal path. The more agile you are, the faster you will take corrective measures to bring yourself back on track.

Finding that one line to summarize all the millions of actions you will take in this life—all the responsibilities you will take up, all the skills you will learn and all the relationships you will build—provides that much-needed focus and clarity.

This central focus will help you to make difficult decisions, choose the ones that best suit you, and clarify how you can continue to make that one line true despite your changing circumstances. It will be your guide and the beacon of light on the dark days. It will calm your mind and settle your heart when you are agitated and distracted.

'Your mind is like this water, my friend; when it is agitated, it becomes difficult to see, but if you allow it to settle, the answer becomes clear.'

Master Oogway, *Kung Fu Panda*

Self-Evaluation

- Think about the brightest moments in your life. What are the common themes in those times?
- Among the common themes, what central idea connects them?
- How does this central idea connect your personal and professional lives?
- What is the one line that will summarize your life?

Your Reflections

Think about the brightest moments in your life. What are the common themes in those times?
Among the common themes, what central idea connects them?
How does this central idea connect your personal and professional lives?
What is the one line that will summarize your life?

37.2. Flow and Steer the Tide

How do salmon defy the current of rivers to swim upstream towards their spawning grounds? Is it by pure force? Their superior skills of leaping and powerful swimming? Or are they aided by their body shape, weight and the size of their tails and fins?

Scientists are still trying to fully understand this phenomenon where salmon and other fish swim upstream, known as rheotaxis. While many questions remain unanswered, there is a general consensus that fish manage to go against the flow by relying on water- and body-motion cues.

A new model has been developed after studying 'the bidirectional hydrodynamic interaction between the fish and the surrounding flow' (Porfiri 2022), which in layperson terms means 'how the presence of the fish alters the flow, which, in turn, affects the fish'.

> Your presence in the ecosystem alters the flow, which, in turn, affects you.

When leaders want to bring about change or are being disrupted in such a way that change becomes necessary, they often face resistance. An understanding of the concept of rheotaxis is helpful in this instance. Too many leaders I know try to beat down tough walls of resistance with brute force, skills (tactical, not strategic), only to get worn down by frustration, eventually.

I remember my conversation with Rachel, a future-oriented middle manager in the healthcare industry, with lots of drive and obvious potential. When she was given the chance to kickstart an innovative change process that would cut across the entire organization, she was thrilled. But problems started emerging as she reached out to other department heads, all of whom outranked her by several levels. Upset that she was meddling in their turf, they thumbed her down and shut their doors firmly in her face. She felt angry at first, then frustrated, and finally defeated. But she did not give up trying. Every time she tried to get a finger hold to pry the doors open, the doors would shut harder than before.

She grew tired and dejected.

I shared the story of the salmon that swam upstream and asked her, 'How do salmon manage to leap against the flow?'

Rachel thought for a moment and then said, 'I am not sure about the science behind it, but I'm sure other than skill and resilience, many other factors have to be in play for the salmon to be able to make the swim.'

The idea of flowing to steer the tide is so important.

As I discovered the phrase that would describe my life and ideal path, I knew the road I wanted to take was against convention. Rachel and I were both leaders striving to swim against the flow. But instead of falling back on our instincts to fight back with even more gusto, how about doing something different instead?

- Flow with circumstances (observe).
- Look beyond the optimal conditions that will shape the flow (evaluate and strategize).
- Grab the opportunities and act at the best possible timing (leap).

Being agile in creating an impact that is aligned with your life's central theme requires you to:

- Immerse yourself in the circumstances.
- Understand the dynamics—where the power flows, what the impediments are.
- Keep the hope to influence alive.
- Not force things to change prematurely.
- Wait or create the right conditions.
- Act at the right time.

Some leaders feel they need to exert control over the outcomes. I agree only to a certain extent because no one can truly guarantee a particular outcome—many things in life are beyond our control. Control is merely an illusion. When we let go of this illusion, we free ourselves to respond to the actual circumstances by observing, evaluating, strategizing, then leaping upstream.

Many leaders are as outcome-oriented as am I. Rachel, too, was outcome-oriented. To obtain the desired outcome, we need to flow better by watching and sensing the trend, then making our move when the time is ripe.

Navigating Rachel's Conundrum

When I asked Rachel why try to break the walls of resistance when it was clear the efforts were futile, it became immediately clear to her based on the overwhelming evidence that the conditions were not right. She could not leap just yet. That was the reality. Instead of forcing her way through, she changed her approach. Instead, she responded by:

- Flowing
- Watching out for signs of opportunity ripening
- Leaping at the right moment

Eventually, through another smaller project with a similar intention, Rachel got the right stakeholders on board and her impact increased. The stakeholders were very happy with the experience of working with her and this smaller project became a prominent success story. The visibility and positive word-of-mouth endorsement it generated softened the department heads' resistance and they began to open their doors to Rachel.

> 'Life is movement. The more life there is, the more flexibility there is. The more fluid you are, the more you are alive.'
>
> Arnaud Desjardins, French author and spiritual teacher

Self-Evaluation

- What are you trying to achieve and not gaining headway at?
- What is aiding you?
- What impediments are there?
- What does the evidence inform you about the relevance of your actions?
- What else can you do instead that might be more productive?

Your Reflections

What are you trying to achieve and not gaining headway at?
What is aiding you?
What impediments are there?
What does the evidence inform you about the relevance of your actions?
What else can you do instead that might be more productive?

37.3. Refresh Your Lens to Get Unstuck

'I always thought the issue was that I wasn't skilful or good enough. But now I realized the issue was never with my actions, but my intentions.'

For nearly seven years, I remained stuck in an unproductive cycle before I decided to take the leadership development programme to upgrade myself. Was there evidence that I was stuck? Plenty. Did I learn from the evidence? Not really.

It did not help that I was surrounded by people who were very similar to me, so they could not provide an alternative perspective either. One day, after some introspection on how terribly downtrodden I felt, a lightning bolt of realization suddenly struck me. I awoke to the painful truth that my issue was not a lack of skills or willingness, but the fact that I was stuck in a broken mindset. The signs were there, but I did not see them.

> *You cannot admire the whole painting if your nose is touching it.*

When things go wrong, people habitually look for causes or others to blame. Often, their perspective is inside-out (a self-oriented perspective) instead of outside-in (how others would perceive them). When your evidence-collection process is always from the same angle, the evidence will unlikely bear new insights, or unveil a different part of the truth.

To prevent yourself from missing the signs and getting stuck, take a different approach. When things don't go according to plan, perform a retrospective and examine the problem with fresh eyes. Think about it in different ways.

Some actions that could help are:

- See it through someone else's eyes.
- Ask allies and stakeholders for their perspectives and thoughts.
- Distance yourself from the problem and look at it again.
- Take a helicopter view (macro level).
- Fast-forward into the future and look back at this moment as if it were in the past (like watching a film).

Self-Evaluation

- How do you measure your life so far?
- What would the past you say?
- What would the future you say?
- What recurring patterns do you notice in your life?

Your Reflections

How do you measure your life so far?
What would the past you say?
What would the future you say?
What recurring patterns do you notice in your life?

37.4. Broaden Your Perspective

What is your natural reaction when you meet someone who has a different perspective? Is it fear or intrigue? Anger or curiosity? Dismissal or acceptance?

A typical theme that emerges in many conversations I have with leaders is the need to achieve a reasonable level of understanding among collaborators. Conceptually, we know that alignment is important, but it is not easy to achieve, especially with a workforce that is increasingly diverse. Naturally, we tend to prefer people who look like us, sound like us and think like us, because it's easy to get along and understand one another.

This thinking, while natural, is one that agile leaders need to watch out for.

Staying with the same group of people, listening to the same perspectives based on similar beliefs can be rewarding, but also confining. When our world expands exponentially in size and complexity, our perspectives also need expand correspondingly. Failing to do so actively limits our worldview to that of the frog in the well.

> 'The frog in the well knows nothing of the sea.'
>
> Japanese proverb

Broadening your perspective helps you to understand the world from different points of view. As you construct a more accurate and up-to-date version of the world in your mind, you will acquire a greater understanding of issues, people, events, cultures and societies. By looking at things through multiple lenses open-mindedly, we can more easily identify solutions to problems or new opportunities for growth. Additionally, broadening perspectives helps us be more inclusive and accepting of those with differing views. It encourages creativity and allows us to learn from a variety of sources. Broadening our perspectives is key to unlocking beneficial new insights.

Some actions that may help include:

- Intentionally mingle with others who have different life experiences and work exposure.
- Prepare a set of questions around topics you are interested to discuss and learn more.
- Find opportunities to collaborate with people who are different from you.

Self-Evaluation

- When was the last time you met someone with a different experience?
- What about the last time you heard a different perspective about an interesting issue?
- How can you expand your circle to increase diversity?

Your Reflections

When was the last time you met someone with a different experience?
What about the last time you heard a different perspective about an interesting issue?
How can you expand your circle to increase diversity?

37.5. Reconnect with a Sense of Wonderment

I once received this training request: 'Chuen Chuen, we have a very strong management team. All of us are highly confident and experts in our areas of expertise. But that is also the cause of our problems. Everybody thinks they are right and insists others must listen to them for they are the authority in their field. As a result, no one is listening. We need help.'

Becoming a strong and confident leader is the goal for many, but how do you know whether you are strong and confident, or just stubborn and arrogant? Being confident involves being sure that you are right. Being arrogant appears to be the same. The difference between a closed and open mind makes a huge difference here.

Arrogance plants the seed of ignorance.

For such training requests, I have to prepare twice as much because I know that for any of my views to be considered, I would need to first convince my highly critical audience that I am credible enough to share something with them. Only then would their minds open to see what I had to offer.

While I understand that such is the natural way of the corporate world, I could not help but wonder if one day, unshakeable confidence would get in the way of some leaders' development. Someday it probably will, but I suspect they may not realize the bus has left until it's been long gone.

I have certainly seen situations where people in senior management arrive at a plateau—the Peter's Plateau. This is not a pleasant situation to be in, for the longer they stay within the system while refusing to learn anything new, the more irrelevant they become. The downstream impact of this for organizations is unfortunate.

I remember fondly the days when I was a teacher. In the classroom, young, hungry minds are always open to receiving information. When they process the information and turn it into knowledge, their faces light up with wonderment. How wonderful growing and evolving can be if there is awe and joy in learning!

If only leaders continue to retain that sense of wonderment, they will grow wiser, their skills will be sharpened and they will remain agile and relevant.

Some actions that may help include:

- Make a list of up-and-coming developments in your industry and learn about them.
- Engage with other experts from your industry or role and hear their views.
- When someone does something you don't expect, ask, 'Tell me more'.

Conclusion

People and strategy are the 'levers' of high-performing organizations. The potential to unlock sound strategies depends on people working in unison to propel organizations to greater heights. The key to activating both levers rests on the shoulders of leaders.

While there are various models of leadership, no single one is superior to another. For leaders who operate in the midst of chaotic business conditions, striving hard to bring order and clarity to the system, the only way to lead effectively and with relevance is to become an agile leader.

The tides have now turned. Shrinking talent pools and diminishing resources combined with the continuous demands to deliver, serve to create a challenge for the leaders of today like never before. They have to fulfil a tall order—getting the most out of a diverse workforce, nurturing them in an empowering culture while fulfilling consumers' growing expectations. It will take more for leaders to lead in the time to come, for they need to earn the right to do so. Past methods where the needs of the followers come second, are no longer viable.

People must be at the heart of organizations in this new era. An excellent strategy is hollow and lifeless if people don't work in unison to realize it. To unleash the full potential of the talent pool, leaders need to re-examine what employees really want. We have to ask ourselves:

- Is the work meaningful and purposeful?
- Is there growth and progression in their careers?
- Do we trust them to do what they do best and develop their strengths?
- Do we care for them as human beings and about nurturing them as a whole person?

Leaders need to figure out what makes the individuals tick and realize that there is no one-size-fits-all solution. We may mentally assent that we need to tailor our styles, but the real challenge lies in adopting a new mindset and putting people's skills to work. Leaders today cannot rely only on good intentions and best efforts, and hope that things will pan out for the best.

Unlocking the secret of happy and fulfilling
workplaces is now in the hands of leaders.

Workplaces of today demand better leaders. The connection between good leadership and happy employees is undeniable. Good leaders make work and lives great. Conversely, bad ones make work and lives miserable. We simply cannot leave it to chance. The well-being of humanity lies within the hands of its leaders. For this reason, we need a sound, attainable framework that introduces new ways of engaging the diverse workforce, while gradually expanding skillsets. It will take time for you to hone these skills and mindsets, but every step you take brings you one step closer to becoming a more agile and relevant leader.

The journey to becoming a leader people love will surely be rewarding. You will leave a legacy and much like the salmon, you will change the water as the water changes you.

Embrace the possibilities. Optimize your strategies. Maximize your impact.

Become a leader people will love.

Acknowledgements

Since I embarked on a disruptive career change in 2017, leaving my stable job as an educator to venture into entrepreneurship and later, to set up an executive coaching and leadership consulting practice, I have met many benefactors to whom I owe my thanks.

In May 2020, I published my first book, *8 Paradoxes of Leadership Agility*, also derived from patterns I have observed from my growing coaching practice. The book received good reception and has since opened many doors for me. With the power of an authentic and relatable brand, social media marketing, and the ability to connect over online networks, I have been able to connect with readers from all over the globe. Many of these relationships have progressed into ongoing partnerships.

The encouragement I received from many of these esteemed partners became a lifeline for me. As an anxious new business owner without a script to follow, I faced many fears and self-doubt—like many leaders of today who are trying to write their rule books. To be seen, recognized, and valued by people of their standing has made all the difference.

Some even became my informal mentors, sharing global business knowledge and further advancing my strategic thinking as I agilely adapted my business strategies for the future. Meeting benefactors and generous business veterans made my experience of 'flying the plane as I build it' (one of my descriptors for leadership agility) exhilarating and rewarding.

I have learned, grown, and evolved on my journey alongside all the leaders who entered my life. Every interaction and well-meaning advice was taken to heart, and they each left an impression, changing me a little each time.

One of the biggest milestones in my new disrupted career was starting my podcast, *Agile Leaders Conversations*. You will find many quotes in this book derived from my guests' nuggets of wisdom and unfiltered golden advice.

LinkedIn was undoubtedly the biggest platform and enabler for me to propagate my voice. This book would not have been possible without the generosity and support of the strangers I have met on LinkedIn, and I thank all of them from the bottom of my heart.

A special mention also goes to my publisher for seeing the light in me—an Asian woman redefining success in a modern world and making her voice heard in the world of leadership.

I am also thankful that you have chosen to pick up this book to include in your leadership development toolkit. I am one step closer to fulfilling my dream and life goal—shaping the future of leadership for the better.

Thank you.

References

ACESENCE Agile Leaders Conversations. 2023. *Agile Leaders Conversations – Insights from Leading Positive Change in the VUCA World.* https://blog.acesence.com/category/agile-leaders-conversations/ (accessed February 2023).

Arbinger Institute. 2018. *Leadership and Self-Deception: Getting out of the Box.* Oakland: Berrett-Koehler Publishers.

Biasutti, Michelle. 2011. 'Flow Theory'. ScienceDirect Topics. https://www.sciencedirect.com/topics/psychology/flow-theory (accessed February 2023).

Binvel, Yannik, Franzino, Michael et al. 2018. 'Future of Work: The Global Talent Crunch'. Korn Ferry. https://www.kornferry.com/content/dam/kornferry/docs/pdfs/KF-Future-of-Work-Talent-Crunch-Report.pdf?ref=hackernoon.com (accessed February 2023).

Bommel, Tara Van. PhD. 2021. *The Power of Empathy in Times of Crisis and Beyond* (Report). Catalyst. https://www.catalyst.org/reports/empathy-work-strategy-crisis (accessed February 2023).

Bonic, Ilya, Carter, Nigel, et al. 2022. 'Rise of the Relatable Organization'. Mercer 2023 Executive Outlook Study. https://www.mercer.com/content/dam/mercer/attachments/private/global-talent-trends/2023/pdf-2023-global-talent-trends-full-report-english-6013195a.pdf (accessed February 2023).

Boyles, Michael. 2022. 'Innovation in Business: What It Is & Why It's so Important'. Business Insights Blog. Harvard Business School. https://online.hbs.edu/blog/post/importance-of-innovation-in-business (accessed February 2023).

Bradberry, Travis and Greaves, Jean. 2009. *Emotional Intelligence 2.0*. San Diego: TalentSmart.

Brickman, Sophie. 21 June 2022. 'When Stressed, We "Catastrophize"— but We Can Learn to Calm Our Irrational Fears'. *The Guardian*. https://www.theguardian.com/commentisfree/2022/jun/21/catastophizing-stress-brain-science (accessed February 2023).

Bromley, Timothy, Lauricella, Taylor and Schaninger, Bill. 2021. 'Making Work Meaningful from the C-Suite to the Frontline'. McKinsey & Company. https://www.mckinsey.com/capabilities/people-and-organizational-performance/our-insights/the-organization-blog/making-work-meaningful-from-the-c-suite-to-the-frontline (accessed February 2023).

Brown, Brené. 2021. *The Anatomy of Trust*. https://brenebrown.com/podcast/the-anatomy-of-trust.

Bungay, Michael. 2016. *The Coaching Habit: Say Less, Ask More; Change the Way You Lead Forever*. Toronto, ON, Canada: Page Two Books, Inc.

Carnegie, Dale, Donna Dale Carnegie and Lowell Thomas. 2022. *How to Win Friends and Influence People: Updated for the next Generation of Leaders*. New York, NY: Simon & Schuster.

Carucci, Ron. 2022. 'To Be a Good Manager, You Have to Be a Good Teacher'. *Harvard Business Review*. https://hbr.org/2022/07/to-be-a-good-manager-you-have-to-be-a-good-teacher (accessed February 2023).

Clifton, Jim and Harter, Jim. 2021. *Wellbeing at Work*. New York: Simon and Schuster.

Covey, Stephen R. 2013. *The 7 Habits of Highly Effective People: Powerful Lessons in Personal Change*. New York: Simon & Schuster.

Covey, Stephen and Merrill, Rebecca. 2018. *The Speed of Trust: The One Thing That Changes Everything*. New York, NY: Free Press.

Criscuolo, Paola, Dahlander, Lunis, et al. 2016. 'Evaluating Novelty: The Role of Panels in the Selection of R&D Projects'. Academy of Management. https://journals.aom.org/doi/abs/10.5465/amj.2014.0861 (accessed February 2023).

Deloitte US. 2021. 'The Deloitte Global Millennial Survey: A decade in review'. Deloitte US. https://www2.deloitte.com/content/dam/Deloitte/global/Documents/2021-deloitte-global-millennial-survey-decade-review.pdf (accessed February 2023).

Desjardins, Jeff. 2019. 'Generation Z: What to Expect from the Newest Addition to the Workforce'. World Economic Forum. https://www.weforum.org/agenda/2019/02/meet-generation-z-the-newest-member-to-the-workforce (accessed February 2023).

Dixon-Fyle, Sundiatu, Dolan, et al. 2020. 'Diversity Wins: How Inclusion Matters'. McKinsey & Company. https://www.mckinsey.com/featured-insights/diversity-and-inclusion/diversity-wins-how-inclusion-matters (accessed February 2023).

Dondi, Marco, Klier, Julia, et al. 2021. 'Defining the Skills Citizens Will Need in the Future World of Work'. McKinsey & Company. https://www.mckinsey.com/industries/public-and-social-sector/our-insights/defining-the-skills-citizens-will-need-in-the-future-world-of-work (accessed February 2023).

Edelman. 2022. 'Edelman Trust Barometer'. Edelman. https://www.edelman.com/trust/2022-trust-barometer (accessed February 2023).

Edelman. 2023. 'Edelman Trust Barometer'. Edelman. https://www.edelman.com/trust/2023-trust-barometer (accessed February 2023).

Eumura, Kenjiro. 2018. *The Fourth Meaning in Life: With a Discussion of What Viktor E. Frankl Calls Meaning*. *Philosophy Study*. 8. https://www.researchgate.net/publication/327958572_The_Fourth_Meaning_in_Life_With_a_Discussion_of_What_Viktor_E_Frankl_Calls_Meaning (accessed February 2023).

Feltman, Charles. 2008. *The Thin Book of Trust: An Essential Primer for Building Trust at Work*. United States of America: Thin Book Publishing.

Frei, Frances and Morriss, Anne. 2020. 'Everything Starts with Trust'. *Harvard Business Review*. https://hbr.org/2020/05/begin-with-trust (accessed February 2023).

Furstenthal, Laura, Morris, Alex and Roth, Erik. 2022. 'Fear Factor: Overcoming Human Barriers to Innovation'. McKinsey & Company. https://www.mckinsey.com/capabilities/strategy-and-corporate-finance/our-insights/fear-factor-overcoming-human-barriers-to-innovation (accessed February 2023).

Gallup, Inc. 2023. *State of the Global Workplace Report*. Gallup. https://www.gallup.com/workplace/349484/state-of-the-global-workplace-2022-report.aspx (accessed February 2023).

Gartner. 2021. 'Gartner Survey Reveals HR Leaders' Number One Priority in 2022 Will Be Building Critical Skills and Competencies'. Gartner. https://www.gartner.com/en/newsroom/press-releases/2021-10-20-gartner-survey-reveals-hr-leaders--number-one-priorit (accessed February 2023).

Gartner. 2023. 'Organizational Change Management: HR Insights'. Gartner. https://www.gartner.com/en/human-resources/insights/organizational-change-management (accessed February 2023).

Goleman, Daniel. 2004. 'What Makes a Leader?'. *Harvard Business Review*. https://hbr.org/2004/01/what-makes-a-leader (accessed February 2023).

Gomez, Karianne, Mawhinney, Tiffany and Betts, Kimberly. 2023. 'Welcome To Generation Z'. Deloitte US. https://www2.deloitte.com/content/dam/Deloitte/us/Documents/consumer-business/welcome-to-gen-z.pdf (accessed February 2023).

Harter, Jim. 2021. 'Manager Burnout Is Only Getting Worse'. Gallup. https://www.gallup.com/workplace/357404/manager-burnout-getting-worse.aspx (accessed February 2023).

Harvard Business Publishing Corporate Learning. 2022. 'When There Is Conflict Among Individuals in Your Organization, How Do They Most Often Respond?'. Harvard Business Publishing Corporate Learning.

Harvard Business Publishing Corporate Learning. 2023. 'Why Conflict Is the Key to Unlocking Innovation Five Critical Behaviors for Navigating Difficult Interactions'. Harvard Business

Publishing Corporate Learning. https://www.harvardbusiness. org/insight/why-conflict-is-the-key-to-unlocking-innovation/ (accessed February 2023).

Hayes, Dr Mary, Chumney, Dr Frances and Buckingham, Marcus. 2020. *Global Workplace Study 2020*. ADP Research Institute. https://www.adpri.org/wp-content/uploads/2020/09/R0130_0920_v3_GWS_ResearchReport.pdf (accessed February 2023).

Jehn, Karen and Shah, Priti Pradhan. 1997. 'Interpersonal relationships and task performance: An examination of mediation processes in friendship and acquaintance groups'. American Psychological Association. https://psycnet.apa.org/record/1997-03701-006 (accessed February 2023).

Kininmonth, Christine. 2021. 'Marcus Buckingham: 4 Ways to Build Resilience'. The Growth Faculty. https://www.thegrowthfaculty. com/blog/leadershipmarcusbuckinghamresilience (accessed February 2023).

Kirsch, Stuart. 2020. 'Running out?: Rethinking Resource Depletion. The extractive industries and society'. U.S. National Library of Medicine. https://www.ncbi.nlm.nih.gov/pmc/articles/PMC734 1033 (accessed February 2023).

Kirsner, Scott. 2018. 'The Most Commonly Cited Barriers to Innovation in Large Companies? Internal Politics'. *Harvard Business Review*. https://hbr.org/2018/07/the-biggest-obstacles-to-innovation-in-large-companies (accessed February 2023).

Krauss, Samantha and Orth, Ulrich. 2021. 'Work Experiences and Self-Esteem Development: A Meta-Analysis of Longitudinal Studies'. *European Journal of Personality*. 36(6). pp. 849–869. https://journals.sagepub.com/doi/full/10.1177/08902070211027142 (accessed February 2023).

Mahto, Monika, Hatfield, Steve, et al. 2022. 'Creating Support for Neurodiversity in the Workplace'. Deloitte Insights. Deloitte. https://www2.deloitte.com/us/en/insights/topics/talent/neurodiversity-in-the-workplace.html (accessed February 2023).

Marcellus, Sibile. 2021. 'Millennials or Gen Z: Who Is Doing the Most Job-Hopping?'. Yahoo! Finance. https://sg.finance.yahoo. com/news/millennials-or-get-z-who-is-doing-the-most-job-hopping-112733374.html (accessed February 2023).

McCarthy, John. 2018. 'Extending the Silence'. George Lucas Educational Foundation. https://www.edutopia.org/article/extending-silence (accessed February 2023).

McKinsey. 2021. 'Losing from Day One: Why Even Successful Transformations Fall Short'. McKinsey & Company. https://www.mckinsey.com/capabilities/people-and-organizational-performance/our-insights/successful-transformations (accessed February 2023).

Morin, Amy. 2020. 'How "Toxic Positivity" at Work May Be Damaging Your Mental Health – And What You Can Do about It, According to a Psychotherapist'. *Business Insider.* https://www.businessinsider.com/how-toxic-positivity-at-work-may-be-damaging-mental-health-2020-11 (accessed February 2023).

O'Boyle, Ed. 2023. '4 Things Gen Z and Millennials Expect from Their Workplace'. Gallup. https://www.gallup.com/workplace/336275/things-gen-millennials-expect-workplace.aspx (accessed February 2023).

O'Brien, Kyle. 2017. 'New Gen Z Study Explains "Pivotal" Generation for Marketers and Brands'. The Drum. https://www.thedrum.com/news/2017/01/26/new-gen-z-study-explains-pivotal-generation-marketers-and-brands (accessed February 2023).

People Management. 2021. *People Management Report.* The Predictive Index. https://www.predictiveindex.com/learn/inspire/resources/surveys-reports/people-management-report (accessed February 2023).

People Management 2022. The State of Talent Optimization 2022. The Predictive Index. https://www.predictiveindex.com/learn/talent-optimization/resources/surveys-reports/the-state-of-talent-optimization (accessed February 2023).

Perlow, Leslie, Hadley, Constance, and Eun, Eunice. 2017. 'Stop the Meeting Madness'. *Harvard Business Review.* https://hbr.org/2017/07/stop-the-meeting-madness (accessed February 2023).

Peter, Laurence J., Hull, Raymond and Sutton, Robert I. 2020. *The Peter Principle: Why Things Always Go Wrong.* London: Profile Books.

Pidgeon, Emily. 2014. The Economic Impact of Bad Meetings. Ideas. Ted.Com. https://ideas.ted.com/the-economic-impact-of-bad-meetings (accessed February 2023).

Pink, Daniel. 2018. *To Sell Is Human: The Surprising Truth About Moving Others*. Edinburgh: Canongate Books.

Porfiri, Maurizio. 2022. 'A Model against the Flow'. eLife Sciences Publications, Ltd. https://elifesciences.org/digests/75225/a-model-against-the-flow (accessed February 2023).

Pursuit of Happiness. 2018. 'Viktor Frankl'. https://www.pursuit-of-happiness.org/history-of-happiness/viktor-frankl (accessed February 2023).

Quillen, Abby. 2020. 'The Workforce's Newest Members: Generation Z'. Zerocater. https://zerocater.com/blog/2018/06/04/workforce-newest-members-generation-z (accessed February 2023).

Robert Bly. 2011. *Kabir: Ecstatic Poems*, Boston: Beacon Press.

Schaninger, Bill, Samo, Jay, et al. 2021. 'Help Your Employees Find Purpose – or Watch Them Leave'. McKinsey & Company. https://www.mckinsey.com/capabilities/people-and-organizational-performance/our-insights/help-your-employees-find-purpose-or-watch-them-leave (accessed February 2023).

Schawbel, Dan. 2022. 'Upskilling Study'. Workplace Intelligence. http://workplaceintelligence.com/upskilling-study (accessed February 2023).

Scott, Kim. 2019. *Radical Candor: Be a Kick-Ass Boss without Losing Your Humanity*. New York: St. Martin's Press.

Smet, Aaron De, Dowling, Bonnie, Hancock, Bryan, and Schaninger, Bill. 2022. 'The Great Attrition Is Making Hiring Harder. Are You Searching the Right Talent Pools?' McKinsey & Company. https://www.mckinsey.com/capabilities/people-and-organizational-performance/our-insights/the-great-attrition-is-making-hiring-harder-are-you-searching-the-right-talent-pools (accessed February 2023).

Smet, Aaron De, Dowling, Bonnie, Hancock, Bryan and Schaninger, Bill. 2022. 'The Great Attrition Is Making Hiring Harder. Are You Searching the Right Talent Pools?'. McKinsey & Company. https://www.mckinsey.com/capabilities/people-and-organizational-performance/our-insights/the-great-attrition-is-making-hiring-harder-are-you-searching-the-right-talent-pools (accessed February 2023).

Smith, Khalil, Grant, Heidi, Rock David. 2019. 'How to Speak up When It Matters'. *Harvard Business Review*. https://hbr.org/2019/03/how-to-speak-up-when-it-matters (accessed February 2023).

Tedeschi, Richard G. 2022. 'Crisis Management: Growth After Trauma'. *Harvard Business Review.* https://hbr.org/2020/07/growth-after-trauma (acces*sed February 2023).*

Thomas, Rick. 2022. 'How to Train Your Flea, or How to Control Others'. Life Over Coffee. https://lifeovercoffee.com/how-to-train-your-flea-also-called-how-to-be-controlled-by-someone (accessed February 2023).

Whillans, Ashley. 2020. *Time Smart: How to Reclaim Your Time and Live a Happier Life.* Boston: Harvard Business Review Press.

Wing, Carey W. 2017. 'The Rising Cost of Resources and Global Indicators of Change'. *American Scientist.* Sigma Xi, The Scientific Research Honor Society. https://www.americanscientist.org/article/the-rising-cost-of-resources-and-global-indicators-of-change (accessed February 2023).

World Economic Forum. 2022. 'The Good Work Framework'. World Economic Forum. https://www3.weforum.org/docs/WEF_The_Good_Work_Framework_2022.pdf (accessed February 2023).

Yeo, Chuen Chuen. 2020. *8 Paradoxes of Leadership Agility.* Singapore: ACESENCE.